HISTORY OF VIETNAMESE COMMUNISM
1925–1976

HISTORIES OF RULING COMMUNIST PARTIES
Richard F. Staar, editor

HISTORY OF VIETNAMESE COMMUNISM, 1925–1976

Douglas Pike

HOOVER INSTITUTION PRESS
Stanford University • Stanford, California

Hoover Institution Publication 189

© 1978 by the Board of Trustees of the
   Leland Stanford Junior University
All rights reserved
International Standard Book Number: 0-8179-6892-X
Library of Congress Catalog Card Number: 77-78051
Printed in the United States of America
Second printing 1979

Contents

PARTY STRUCTURE OF THE SOCIALIST REPUBLIC OF VIETNAM

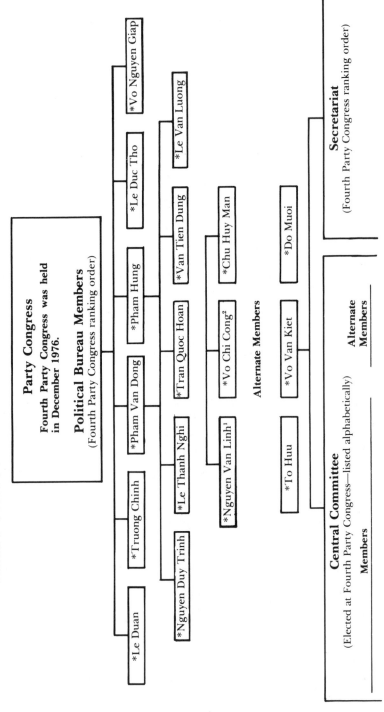

Party Congress

Fourth Party Congress was held in December 1976.

Political Bureau Members

(Fourth Party Congress ranking order)

*Le Duan *Truong Chinh *Pham Van Dong *Pham Hung *Le Duc Tho *Vo Nguyen Giap

*Nguyen Duy Trinh *Le Thanh Nghi *Tran Quoc Hoan *Van Tien Dung *Le Van Luong

*Nguyen Van Linh[1] *Vo Chi Cong[2] *Chu Huy Man

Alternate Members

*To Huu *Vo Van Kiet *Do Muoi

Central Committee

(Elected at Fourth Party Congress—listed alphabetically)

Members

Alternate Members

Secretariat

(Fourth Party Congress ranking order)

†Hoang Anh
†Le Duc Anh
†Tran Ngoc Ban
†Nguyen Luong Bang
†Dang Quoc Bao
†Nguyen Thanh Binh
†Hoang Cam
†Nguyen Van Chi
†Duong Quoc Chinh
*Truong Chinh
†Nguyen Con
*Vo Chi Cong[2]
†Phan Van Dang[4]
†Le Quang Dao
†Nguyen Thi Dinh
†Tran Do
†Ngo Duy Dong
*Pham Van Dong
†Tran Dong
†Vo Thuc Dong
*Le Duan
†Tran Huu Duc
*Van Tien Dung
†La Lam Gia
*Vo Nguyen Giap
†Song Hao
†Le Van Hien
†Tran Van Hien
†Le Quang Hoa
*Tran Quoc Hoan
*Pham Hung
†Nguyen Xuan Huu
*To Huu
†Tran Quang Huy

†Dang Huu Khiem
†Nguyen Huu Khieu
†Doan Khue
†Pham Van Kiet
*Vo Van Kiet
†Hoang Van Kieu
†Nguyen Lam
†Nguyen Quang Lam
†Vu Lap
†Nguyen Thanh Le
†Tran Le
†Vu Dinh Lieu
*Nguyen Van Linh[1]
†Vu Ngoc Linh
†Tran Van Long
*Le Van Luong
†Nguyen Huu Mai
*Chu Huy Man
†Truong Minh
*Do Muoi
*Le Thanh Nghi
†Dong Sy Nguyen
†Nguyen Thi Nhu
†Le Van Nhung
†Do Van Nuong
†Le Van Pham
†Bui Phung
†Ha Thi Que
†Nguyen Quyet
*Tran Quynh
†Tran Sam
†Bui San
†Phan Ngoc Sen

†Tran Van Som
†Nguyen Tuan Tai
†Nguyen Duc Tam
†Ha Ke Tan
†Le Trong Tan
†Bui Quang Tao
†Nguyen Co Thach
†Hoang Van Thai
†Le Quoc Than
†Ton Duc Thang
†Ta Hong Thanh
†Vo Van Thanh
†Nguyen Thi Thap
†Dang Thi
†Hoang Minh Thi
†Dinh Duc Thien
*Le Duc Tho
†Nguyen Thanh Tho
†Mai Chi Tho
†Nguyen Duc Thuan
†Xuan Thuy
†Tran Van Tra
*Nguyen Duy Trinh
†Nguyen Ngoc Triu
†Dam Quang Trung
†Tran Nam Trung[3]
†Vu Tuan
†Phan Trong Tue
†Hoang Tung
†Nguyen Thi Bach Tuyet
†Hoang Quoc Viet
†Nguyen Vinh
†Nguyen Nhu Y

†Nguyen Chan
†Cao Dang Chiem
†Do Chinh
†Nguyen Van Chinh
†Nguyen Ngoc Cu
†Y Ngong Niek Dam
†Nguyen Dang
†Tran Huu Du
†Tran Hanh
†Le Ngoc Hien
†Dang Vu Hiep
†Hoang Van Hieu
†Vu Thi Hong
†Le Khac
†Truong Van Kien
†Bui Thanh Khiet
†Tran Lam
†Nguyen Tuong Lan
†Y Mot
†Luong Van Nghia
†Ho Nghinh
†Vu Oanh
†Tran Phuong
†Nguyen Van Si
†Hoang Minh Thao
†Hoang The Thien
†Le Phuoc Tho
†Nguyen Huu Thu
†Le Van Tri
†Nguyen Dinh Tu
†Dao Duy Tung
†Tran Vy

Secretary General
*Le Duan

Members

*Le Duc Tho	†Xuan Thuy
*Nguyen Duy Trinh	†Nguyen Lam
*Nguyen Van Linh	†Song Hao
*To Huu	†Le Quang Dao

Central Committee Departments

Central Control Committee
(Listed in Fourth Party Congress ranking order)

Chairman
Song Hao

Members

†Tran Van Som	Hoang Nguyen Cuong
†Nguyen Van Chi	Pham Chanh
Ngo Thuyen	Nguyen Thi Thanh
Pham Van So	Phan Thi Tot
Nguyen Thanh	Duong Thi Hong Phuong

Central Military Party Committee

Secretary	Deputy Secretary
*Vo Nguyen Giap	*Van Tien Dang
	†Song Hao

*Members of Political Bureau
†Members and Alternate Members of Central Committee

*Listed in order of appearance in 3–4 July 1976 issue of Party daily Nhan Dan.

[1]Also known as Nguyen Van Cuc
[2]Also known as Vo Toan
[3]Also known as Tran Luong
[4]Also known as Hai Van

Editor's Foreword

Douglas Pike's study on the history of North Vietnam's Communist Party is the second in a series of monographs on the histories of the sixteen ruling communist parties from their organization to the present time. The studies were initiated to fill an important gap in the modern English-language historiography on communism in Albania, Bulgaria, Cambodia, China, Cuba, Czechoslovakia, (East) Germany, Hungary, (North) Korea, Laos, Mongolia, Poland, Romania, the Soviet Union, Vietnam, and Yugoslavia.

Each volume in the series covers some of the following aspects of Communist party history.

- Circumstances of founding; early leading personnel; social composition of membership; initial impact on domestic political life.

- Inter-war party situation emphasizing relations with the Comintern (interference in internal party affairs; participation of party cadres in different comintern schools; purges of these cadres at home and in the Soviet Union).

- Positions taken and activities during World War II (attitude during the Stalin-Hitler pact; resistance movement and cooperation with other groups; relations toward Moscow before and after Comintern dissolution).

- Stages on the road to power (changes in leadership and composition of membership; electoral participation and results; methods of settling accounts with political allies and adversaries).

- Stalinist phase and purges after World War II.

- Aspects of de-Stalinization and its impact on party relations with the CPSU; same in domestic political and socio-economic affairs.

- Party problems in the late 1970s, with a final overview of the
- historical role played by the Communist party, its functions in domestic politics (revolutionary transformation of the country) and in the multi-faceted relations with the CPSU.

As general editor of the series, I am pleased that such a distinguished scholar as Mr. Douglas Pike accepted our invitation to prepare this History of the Communist Party in North Vietnam.

Richard F. Staar
Director, International Studies
Hoover Institution
Stanford University

Introduction

This is a history of the Communist Party in Vietnam from its inception in 1930. It is not an analysis of the political dynamics either of the Vietnamese scene or of Vietnamese communism, nor is it a study of the contemporary—which is to say post–Vietnam War—communist movement, although both of these are worthy subjects and, in fact are badly in need of, book-length treatment. Rather, this is a history of the Party only—its organization, its development, its successes and failures, its external relationships—and a tentative assessment of its role in the history of Vietnam.

In the long, winding river of Vietnamese history, there are four currents that relate to the rise of communism in that country, four major historical experiences that formed the milieu that shaped the men who created Vietnamese communism. If space permitted, they would be discussed in detail. They can only be noted here in passing:

* A heritage of traditionalism, which left behind a special kind of social organizational structure and allegiance to a peculiar style of politics.

* A heritage of colonialism, which left a warped economic condition and deep psychological scars.

* The spirit of *doc lap* ("independence"), which produced not only profound resentment against foreign control but also a distorted sense of Vietnam's relations with the external world.

* The turbulent social scene and deep political malaise in Vietnam in the years immediately prior to the birth of Vietnamese communism.

It would be useful to begin with a skeletal outline of the history of Marxism-Leninism in Indochina, in other words, with a brief summary of what is to follow.

The movement grew out of anticolonial nationalist sentiment, which was ever present after French arrival in strength about the time of the American Civil War but which developed significant force around the turn of the century. This anticolonial movement early divided into two elements, the Nationalists and the Communists, and the early years were dominated by the Nationalists. Their struggle involved ideology but was primarily organizational. The Marxist movement, as a serious enterprise, began in the late 1920s, initially as three factions: the Stalinists, the Trotskyists, and a youth-oriented indigenous Marxist group. The first Party, the Indochinese Communist Party, was founded on Comintern orders by Ho Chi Minh in 1930. The 1930s were relatively quiescent ones for the Party, partly because of organizational weakness and partly because of image difficulties created by the united-front tactic that worldwide communism was employing to oppose European fascism. The Party took on steadily increasing importance, however, beginning in late World War II. It seized power in Hanoi in the chaotic days immediately following the end of the war and the departure of the occupying Japanese.

Under the leadership of Ho Chi Minh, aided by a corps of well-trained, mostly middle-class, cadres, the Party took over the anti-French colonial struggle known as the Viet Minh War. It was an accomplishment of superior organization and skillful use internally of the united-front technique. The period, and the war, ended with the 1954 Geneva Conference in which the Party, subordinating its interests to international communism, was partially cheated of the fruits of victory. These were the crucible years, the ones that shaped the Party into the form it retains to this day.

In 1954 the Party came to power in the North. Its first task was to consolidate that power, which it succeeded in doing after a year of difficulty and challenge. Then it set about to achieve three major goals: socialist economic development of the North, unification of the North and South, and transformation of the Vietnamese society into a Marxist model. The first of these was held in abeyance while the third was accomplished in the North and the second—in the form of the Vietnam War—carried forward in the South, eventually to complete success. These tasks were pursued parallel to the maintenance of a complex relationship with the world communist movement, a relationship primarily involving the Chinese and Soviets, and were aided by the Sino-Soviet dispute. Pursuit was also facilitated by the sociopolitical change and turbulence elsewhere in the world, particularly in the United States in the 1960s.

This work is being completed at a time of fundamental transition for Vietnamese communism. Clearly the major task now facing the Party is economic development. But of nearly equal importance are three other major concerns: integration of the South into the whole system, reordering external relations both with its Southeast Asian neighbors and with the rest of the communist world, and managing that cluster of sociopsychological difficulties that the Party collectively calls the quality of socialist life. Complicating these tasks is the imminent generational change of leadership, the average age of the Party's top leadership now being sixty-seven. All of this will have the net effect of unleashing forces of change within the Party, the nature and direction of which can only be dimly perceived.

The system that communism brought to Vietnam, despite its alien genesis, has now become authentically Vietnamese and well rooted in the soil of earlier Vietnamese culture. It cannot be explained by making comparisons with other societies, and it is a trap for those who attempt this. Because it is indigenously Vietnamese, the system would not work elsewhere and thus is no model for others. Whatever else, it is a system without personal freedom—the right of the individual to think as he wishes, to become what he wants to become, or to abstain from acting if he so chooses. Perhaps, as many suggest (and not only Marxists) this sort of personal freedom is fast becoming a luxury that no society anywhere can afford. If this is the case, we can look at Vietnam and see the future. Whether it is a future that works, or ought to work, is in the final analysis a judgment that each must make for himself.

A word on source materials. Of the three types of available materials—those published by Hanoi, accounts by defectors and others who quit the communist side, and works by foreign visitors to Hanoi—only the first has been of value. Defectors can supply bits and pieces of valuable information (especially biographical), but their judgment is not to be trusted. Accounts by short-term visitors, I have found in fifteen years of examination, are virtually worthless. But official materials generally have proven to be informative and reliable (although not comprehensive) if one learns the secret of reading them correctly, which requires understanding the special definitions employed and the unique perception that is the point of departure. Communist propaganda, unlike fascist propaganda, is not calculated lies; it is a kind of truth (with its own terminology and its own world view) that should be taken seriously as a source of information.

This work is the product of some fifteen years of studying Vietnamese communism, most of it in Vietnam. It has been aided by countless Vietnamese friends and associates to whom I am indebted more than words can say. Also, I am deeply indebted to my wife, Myrna, for much valuable advice and assistance. Finally I am grateful to my employers, the U.S. Department of State and the U.S. Information Agency, for allowing me to take the several months' leave necessary to write this book.

Washington, D.C.
January 1977

Chapter 1

The Birth of
Vietnamese Communism

Vietnamese communism was born, if so amorphous a development as a modern mass movement has a fixed time and place of birth, in Canton in 1925.[1]

Although it was a historic moment, there in south China, it was only recognized in retrospect that a fundamental change had occurred in Vietnamese history, the mantle of destiny passed from Vietnamese reformer to Vietnamese revolutionary. The first generation of anti-colonialists, who had so largely determined the degree and kind of opposition offered the French, was fading from the scene, its doctrine in disgrace, its organizational techniques now scorned. Phan Boi Chau was in jail, Phan Chau Trinh was dead—typical fates of the initial leaders. Vietnamese radicals of all stripes, many of whom were living in Canton at the moment, suffered varying degrees of disillusionment over the failure of the cause to advance much under the banners of the Tan Viet, the Tam Tam Xa, and lesser groups then in operation.[2]

It was a propitious moment for the arrival on the scene of a new figure representing a new force in world history. He was a well-traveled, Moscow-trained communist revolutionary, experienced beyond his years. And he arrived in Canton with the authority of a full Comintern agent able to claim as a base of power both the USSR and the Communist Party apparatus in south China. He was the man the world came to know as Ho Chi Minh.[3] Assigned as a liaison agent in the Comintern mission to the Kuomintang (KMT) of China, to work directly under the even then legendary Mikhail Borodin, Ho's orders were to begin a systematic and intensive effort to develop a communist movement in Indochina, using as his nucleus the various Vietnamese émigré radicals in Canton.

THANH NIEN

Ho was a wise choice in such a venture. Boldly he struck out in new organizational directions and created the first of what proved to be a long succession of complex, involuted, overlapping structures, yet with an unchanging essence. This first structure had three elements.

The first was the Oppressed Asian People's Association (Bi Ap Buc Dan Toc Lien Hiep Hoi), what today would be called a communist-led mass organization. Its cofounder was the famed early Indian communist figure, M. N. Roy. The association was designed to be Asian-wide and to include Koreans, Chinese, Indochinese, Indians, and Indonesians. It apparently reflected a grandiose Comintern ambition to create a pan-Asian (or Nan Yang/South Seas) Communist movement.[4] The association, as well as the broader Comintern effort, came to little. It was broken up by police in the respective countries; it never did get the support required to make it a success; and it lasted only a few years. This was Ho's first experiment in united fronts and served, if nothing else, to help school him.

The second element was the (Vietnamese) Young Revolutionary Youth League (Thanh Nien Cach Mang Dong Chi Hoi, originally without the term dong chi), or Thanh Nien for short. It was not a communist party nor a simple front organization but something of both, a nationalist-socialist movement (as Ho described it) incorporating certain party organizational techniques. It was never large, numbering perhaps 50 at the time of its formation, 300 by 1928, and 1,000 by 1930. Two-thirds of its members were in Vietnam, the rest in China.

The third element was an informal but disciplined inner group, the Communist Youth League (Thanh Nien Cong San Doan), which was the beginning of the Party. Official Party history puts it this way:

> In December 1924 Ho came to China. In 1925 he set up the Bi Ap Buc Dan Toc Lien Hiep Hoi and established relations with the Tam Tam Xa, an organization of Vietnamese revolutionaries residing in China, using this agency as a base for founding the Viet Nam Thanh Nien Cach Mang

Dong Chi Hoi. At the same time Ho organized the Cong San Doan within the Thanh Nien as a step toward the creation of a genuine Communist Party of Vietnam.[5]

At the time of its formation, the Thanh Nien Cong San Doan consisted of Ho and six to eight youths. Even later it was only a lateral organization, that is, a cluster of communist cells made up of select members from the Thanh Nien working through that organization and reporting directly to Ho Chi Minh. It was the proto–Communist Party of Vietnam.

This two-tier arrangement—that is, half Party and half non-Party—was dictated by Ho's estimate, one shared by the Comintern, that Vietnam was too backward for a regular communist party. Reportedly Ho argued in Moscow in the summer of 1927 against formation of a communist party in Vietnam on the grounds that no one in Vietnam understood the word *communism.* Deception apparently was not part of his purpose, for Ho at that time was embracing the idea of communism publicly. For example, in the May 1926 issue of *Thanh nien* (the organization's official publication) he wrote that "only a communist party can assure the [eventual] well-being of Annam [i.e., Vietnam]."

Of course, the wheel-within-a-wheel arrangement did permit a more sharply disciplined and orthodox approach both to doctrine and to organization because, as Ho expressed it, in the "Cong San Doan were comrades properly ideologically armed."

The two-tier arrangement also became geographic. Head and body were born in Canton. It was necessary to transplant the body to Indochina and graft onto it all available local revolutionary sentiment. The head remained abroad and would stay there for another decade and a half.

Far more than the various nationalist movements, then, communism came to Vietnam as an import, the result of alien initiative. As an institution it was conceived outside Vietnam, launched from foreign soil, managed from abroad during its formative years and, to a degree, fostered and sustained by interests largely irrelevant to Vietnam.

The last half of the 1920s were busy years for Ho and the Thanh Nien. Activities included:

* A school for revolutionaries in Canton, which by 1929 had trained a corps of some 250 communist cadres. The Thanh Nien also used the facilities of the Whampoa Military Academy (where Ho occasionally

lectured), with its special Vietnam section, which provided excellent training and education.

* Underground movements established in Indochina and Thailand, staffed by some of the Canton-trained cadres. Other Thanh Nien cadres organized cells in the Haiphong cement plant, the Vinh railway workshops, and the Nam Dinh textile plant and on the larger rubber plantations to the South. Thanh Nien members infiltrated French colonial institutions. Party organization followed in the wake. The first Party cell in Hanoi was established in March 1929 by Tran Van Cung. Meanwhile, other cadres in south China set up liaison arrangements with the Chinese Communist Party.

* Extensive agitation and propaganda work in Indochina, particularly staging mass meetings and running protest demonstrations. The Thanh Nien published its own materials and also distributed French Communist Party literature. Major themes employed were antireformism, the necessity of world revolution, and USSR advocacy. Articles were oriented toward the urban worker.

Major figures in the Thanh Nien, who also were members of the inner core of the Communist Youth League, were (in roughly descending order of importance):

* Ho Chi Minh.

* Ho Tung Mau, former Tam Tam Xa leader, chairman of the Thanh Nien until his imprisonment in 1928. Later he escaped, going on to help form the Indochinese Communist Party (ICP) and to become an important figure in the Viet Minh. He was killed during an air attack in 1950 while on an inspection tour.

* Tran Phu (or Tran Phu Thao or Li Kwei), originally a Tan Viet from Ha Tinh, a senior member of the early apparatus. Trained in Moscow in the 1920s, he became a Thanh Nien—Comintern courier and was the first secretary general of the newly formed ICP. He died in prison in September 1931, at age twenty-seven, allegedly tortured to death by his jailers.

* Lam Duc Thu (Nguyen Cong Vien), chairman of the Thanh Nien after Ho Tung Mau's arrest. Party history states he betrayed the Thanh

Nien in 1926, then the Party in 1930 (by giving information to the authorities). He returned to his native village and abandoned politics and was reported executed on Party orders in 1950 to prevent a third betrayal.

* Le Hong Phong, ex–Tam Tam Xa leader who became a major figure in the ICP in the 1930s. Moscow-trained, under the name of Litvinof, he became chairman of the Overseas Leading Communist Committee (sometimes called the Overseas Communist Directorate), which was based in Macao in the early 1930s and briefly ran the Party in Vietnam. Active in Party work in the South during the late 1930s, he was arrested in 1939 by the French and died on Poulo Condor Island prison, September 1942.

* Pham Kiet (Pham Quang Khanh), early Thanh Nien organizer, later an active and prominent Party official. Eventually he became political commissar of the Democratic Republic of Vietnam's Public Security Forces, with the rank of lieutenant general. He died in 1975 at the age of sixty-three.

* Le Hong Son (Hong Son), ex–Tam Tam Xa official who played an important role in Thanh Nien affairs in early years. He was executed by the French in 1933.

* Phung Chi Kien, Thanh Nien organizer who became active in Party affairs in the 1930s. He was elected a member of the ICP Central Committee in 1935. Member of an early guerrilla unit, he was killed in a raid in Bac Son in 1941.

* Ha Huy Tap, active in early organizational work, then went to Moscow for training (under the name Sinikine). He was elected a member of the ICP Central Committee in 1935 and is believed to have been executed by the French in 1941.

* Ngo Gia Tu (Ngo Si Quyet), an early Party organizer in the Hanoi area, working chiefly in military camps and among the urban proletariat. He directed the ICP apparat in the Hanoi region, 1929–30. He was jailed in 1930 and reportedly killed in 1935 (aged thirty) while trying to escape from Poulo Condor Island prison.

* Nguyen Thi Minh Khai, one of the few women active in the early Vietnamese radical/communist movement. She is believed to have

been a Thanh Nien organizer. Her mentor was Tran Phu, later Le Duan. She went to Moscow in 1935 as an ICP Central Committee member and during World War II was secretary general of the ICP Nam Bo Central Committee. Arrested early in the war, she died in prison a few years later. She was Vo Nguyen Giap's first wife.

* Tran Huy Lieu, cofounder of the Thanh Nien organization in the South. He was jailed by the French for much of the 1930s. He edited the Viet Minh newspaper *Cuu quoc,* was first minister of information (1945) of the Democratic Republic of Vietnam (DRV) and later an important figure in Party agitprop work, and was said to be closely associated with Vo Nguyen Giap.

* Other early Thanh Nien members about whom little is known are Le Duy Diem, Luu Quoc Long, Le Thuat Hung, Le Quang Dat, Truong Van Lenh, Le Van Huan, Tran Dinh Thanh, Nguyen Van Cu, and Le Manh Trinh.

Individuals who had some association with the Thanh Nien and went on to become prominent Communist officials include Le Duan, Pham Van Dong, Nguyen Luong Bang, and apparently Truong Chinh.

During its first years the Thanh Nien enjoyed KMT support, although there were reports of Ho's group competing with KMT agents for influence in the Oppressed Asian People's Association. But with the KMT–Chinese Communist breach, and particularly after the abortive three-day Canton Commune episode in December 1927, the KMT turned hostile, suspecting correctly that Thanh Nien members had close associations with, if not dual membership in, the Chinese Communist Party. The Thanh Nien headquarters fled Canton, moving first to rural Kwangsi province and then, in 1929, to Hong Kong. Ho returned to Moscow.

DOCTRINE AND DISINTEGRATION

By 1930 the Vietnamese proto–Communist movement had on its rolls 250–300 cadres, plus 1,300–1,500 members or close collaborators. This organizational force was concentrated (70 percent of the strength) in Tonkin (the North), chiefly in the two cities of Hanoi and Haiphong and the three provinces of Nam Dinh, Thai Binh, and Bac Ninh. It was weaker (20 percent) in Annam (the Center), existing there mainly in the city of Hue and the province of Binh Dinh. Activity (10 percent) in Cochin China (the South) centered around the three major cities of Saigon, My Tho, and Can Tho.

But the Thanh Nien was disintegrating. This was due chiefly to ever-widening fissures—triggered by personality clashes and doctrinal differences—in the cadre corps and in the rank and file. Absence of the strong guiding figure of Ho Chi Minh was also a contributing factor. A third reason was geographic regionalism, the influence among members of the ever-present North-Center-South sense of identification.

At the time of its formation, the Thanh Nien was a group in fairly close doctrinal harmony. Its chief theoretical guide was Lenin. His theory of imperialism adequately explained the Indochinese situation to most Thanh Nien followers. Ho added his own ideological contribution, *Revolutionary Road* (1925). His major points:

* The revolution must have a proletarian, mass base; the worker is the unit, the city the vortex (the peasant was yet to be brought to center stage).

* Marxist-Leninist organizational principles must be employed, that is, organization stressed over personalized leadership, the vanguard principle, the party as elite, the central committee–cell hierarchical structure.

* All policies must conform to the wishes of the Third International.

This last principle never was acceptable to all members and eventually became a chief cause of the Thanh Nien's collapse. Within the question of obedience to proletarian internationalism three specific doctrinal disputes developed.

Which comes first, the world revolution or the national revolution, and which should be favored in the allocation of resources? The Comintern held for the former. Involved here was the issue of emancipation of Vietnam versus development of a worldwide class struggle.

Should the revolution be one-stage or two-stage? The Comintern held for two-stage: first comes the bourgeois democratic revolution that wins independence from colonial rule, then the socialist revolution against the bourgeois democratic regime.

What is the proper relationship of the movement to less radical organizations, particularly to non-Communist revolutionary groups?

Beneath the doctrinal debate was a deeper consideration: the general sense—shared mostly by those who came to be known as the Tonkin Group—of the current of historical development. In the past half decade, it was said, some members had developed along progressive lines and had become increasingly proletarian-minded; others had not moved in this direction and were as bourgeois as ever. Further, because of parochialism, some members did not (and could not) adjust to the mandatory imposition of Comintern discipline. The future belonged to the centrally directed, proletarian-based revolutionary; the failure in the Thanh Nien was that some members simply could not see the road down which Vietnam was traveling.

An effort to heal this doctrinal breach, doomed before it began, was made at the Thanh Nien congress in Hong Kong in May 1929. Rather than unifying the membership, it set loose forces that resulted in a three-way split of the Vietnamese proto-communist movement.

The Indochinese Communist Party (Dong Duong Cong San Dang) was officially proclaimed in June 1929. This was the Tonkin Group, based in Hanoi, urban-centered and industrial-worker-oriented. It set out to be a classic by-the-book communist movement. Major figures included Ngo Gia Tu, Nguyen Van Tuan, Tran Van Cung, Trinh Dinh Cuu, Nguyen Phong Sac, Quoc Anh, Do Ngoc Du, and Tran Tu Thinh (Bang Phong). It published *Bua liem* (Hammer and Sickle) for rank and file, *Bon-se-vich* (Bolshevik) for cadres, and *Co do* (Red Flag) as organ of the Red Trade Union composed of urban proletarians.

The ACP, the Annam Communist Party (Annam Cong San Dang), was formed, a creation of the original Thanh Nien Central Committee (whose leaders for a period operated under both flags). Smaller and less proletarian in composition than the ICP, it was led mostly by teachers and intellectuals. Also, it was more indigenous and less émigré in character than the ICP. It published *Do* (Red Journal) and a newspaper, *Bon-se-vich* (Bolshevik).

The ICL, the Indochinese Communist League, or Alliance (Dong Duong Cong San Lien Doan), also arose. It included some Thanh Nien residue but was mainly a continuation of the militant Tan Viet. Its major figure was Tran Phu, and its members were mostly students and teachers; thus it was more bourgeois than either the ICP or the ACP. For several years the ICL and its predecessor organizations[6] represented a separate stream of rather impure communist thought, or, as Ho Chi Minh expressed it, having only Marxist tendencies. Through the 1920s, however, this element maintained close relations with Ho; in fact, most of its cadres were trained by him. Doctrinally, the ICL was more utopian and in some ways more bloody-handed than either the ICP or the ACP.[7]

Both the ICP and the ACP sought the Comintern seal of approval and each tried to get Ho Chi Minh to plead its case. The Comintern, after issuing a patronizing criticism of the existing factionalism, ordered Ho to Hong Kong to effect a unification and upgrading of the Indochinese communist movement.

Thus in 1929 there existed three Communist organizations, each of which claimed to be a genuine revolutionary party of the working class and all of which were trying by all means to win recognition by international communism. . . . Confronted with this situation, the Communist International sent a letter to the communists in Indochina pointing out the necessity of ending division and sectarianism and of fusing into a united Communist Party. To implement the instructions of the Communist International, Comrade Nguyen Ai Quoc [Ho Chi Minh] went to Hong Kong to convene the delegates of the Communist organizations in Indochina to discuss the question of unification of the Party.[8]

The Comintern directive (October 27, 1929) that ordered the formation of the ICP officially determined that Indochina was ready for a normal communist party.

Divisions among various Communist groups . . . cannot be tolerated. . . . The most urgent important task of all Communists in Indochina is to form a revolutionary party with a proletarian class base, that is, a popular Communist Party of Indochina. It should be the only Communist organization in Indochina. . . .

The Indochina Communist Party should bring together all Communist groups. To achieve this aim, we should form immediately, under the leadership of a representative from the Executive Committee of the Comintern, an intergroup committee composed of representatives of all organizations recognizing the principle, regulations, and resolutions of the Comintern and working actively among the workers and people. . . . Problems will be tackled under the supervision of the representative of the Comintern Executive Committee and the solutions to these problems will be carried out only when they have been approved by the representative of the Comintern Executive Committee. . . . Only the groups and organizations which completely approve the resolutions of the Comintern Executive Committee and the Communist International can be recognized as organs of the Indochinese Communist Party and can send their representatives to the Party congress. . . . All organizations and individuals who do not recognize the resolutions of the Comintern must be expelled from the Party.[9]

The Comintern's position was that the Thanh Nien's indecisiveness and lack of self-discipline was engendering disunity, the movement's greatest danger. It asserted that objective conditions for a capitalist revolution did exist in Vietnam and that the consciousness of the workers there had been raised to a level such that creation of a communist party was not only possible but urgently required. Actually, it is not clear whether the Comintern ordered formation because it truly believed Indochina was ready for a regular party or simply saw it as the best means of ending organizational disarray and competition. The Comintern did make it clear who was the wooer and who the wooed, setting down twenty-one conditions to be met before the proposed party would be admitted into the world communist fraternity.[10]

THE PARTY IS BORN

The historic unification conference began in a soccer stadium in Hong Kong (some reports place it in a rural Kowloon barn) on January 6, 1930, and lasted several weeks. Ho Chi Minh presided, and attending were about a dozen individuals representing the ICP and the ACP. The ICL was not present officially, although apparently some of its members were. The Vietnam Communist Party (Vietnam Cong San Dang) was formed with a chapter membership of 211, according to official history; this included 85 members from the ICP or Tonkin Group, 61 from the ACP, 11 from the ICL, and 54 other Vietnamese communists living abroad, mainly in Canton and Hong Kong.

The results of the conference and the actions that followed it were these:

* It unified the disparate organizational elements into a single, formal communist party, proclaimed the Vietnam Communist Party on February 3, 1930. It established a nine-man Central Committee with Tran Phu as secretary general.

* It integrated the Vietnamese communist movement into the regional and worldwide communist system and arranged a formal liaison

mechanism. At the lowest (or national) level, the Party was equal to the Siam and Malay Communist parties. These three were coordinated laterally by the Comintern's Southern Bureau in Singapore, which administratively was under the Comintern Far Eastern Bureau in Shanghai. The Shanghai Bureau reported directly to the Communist International (Comintern) in Moscow.[11]

* It arranged the Party's incorporation into the network of international front and collaborationist organizations, chiefly those involving trade unions. The primary organization in Asia for this activity was the Pan-Pacific Trade Union, a communist front headquartered in Shanghai, submember of the Red International of Labor Unions of Moscow. This front linkage also involved connections with the Unitaire Confederation Generale du Travail (Unitary CGT) in Paris. The Unitary CGT was an arm of the French Communist Party, hence there was established early a strong and in some ways peculiar connection between the communist parties of Indochina and France.

* Internally, it created a network of overlapping front and mutual-interest organizations, an institutional approach that was to become a Ho Chi Minh hallmark. These included the National United Front against Imperialism (Mat Tran Dan Toc Thong Nhat Chong De Quoc), the smaller Antiimperialist League (Hoi Dong Minh Phan De), the Red Peasant Association (Nong Hoi Do), the Women's Liberation Association (Hoi Phu Nu Giai Phong), the Party youth organization formed in Saigon on March 31, 1931, and initially called the Communist Youth Group (Thanh Nien Cong San Doan), plus a welter of of basic-level elements: assistance associations; organizations of workers, small traders, and owners of small industrial concerns; sports and training associations; reading societies; harvest, rice-transplanting, and roof-rethatching teams; burial societies; hunting and fishing clubs; feasting societies (during Tet), and others.

* It received and ratified Ho Chi Minh's famous "Political platform and outline of strategy" (Chinh cuong sach luoc van tat), a philosophic rather than program-oriented outline of future Party policy. The sense of it had already been conveyed in pamphlet form in mid-1929:

> The Party line is to carry out a democratic bourgeois revolution, including a land revolution, in order to topple the French imperialists and the feudal elements, make Viet Nam totally independent, and move forward to socialism and communism. In order to successfully carry out that

line, it is necessary to build up the Party of the working class, to build the worker-peasant army, to achieve the worker-peasant alliance, and to establish the National United Front, and it is necessary for the Vietnamese revolution to unite with the world revolutionary movement.[12]

* It arranged for systematic financial support for the movement, soon including an annual Comintern appropriation of about $25,000 (U.S. equivalent) per year.

* It ordered the formation of a newspaper, *Tien len* (Forward), which became the initial Party organ and was distributed widely during the crucial years of 1931 and 1932.

* In sum, the conference, in the official view, unleashed a new force in Indochina.

> Like all Communist Parties the world over, the Viet Nam Communist Party was a new-type party of the working class armed with Marxism-Leninism. It was the most advanced, most politically enlightened, and at the same time the highest organization of the Vietnamese working class, fully able to lead the other organizations of the Vietnamese working class and people.[13]

The Comintern was not entirely satisfied. Being oriented toward pan-Asianism rather than toward national-level communism, it was particularly displeased with the parochial choice of name: the Vietnam Communist Party.

> After studying the documents of the Unification Meeting, the Communist International immediately sent a letter with instructions to the Viet Nam Communist Party amending a number of points in the line and tasks of the Vietnamese revolution and with suggestions about the question of changing the Party's name to Indochinese Communist Party.[14]

In response—and apparently over the demur of Ho Chi Minh, for whom this represented a political setback—the Party Central Committee met in October 1930 and changed the official name to Indochinese Communist Party (Dang Cong San Dong Duong). Thereupon, it was granted national section status by the Comintern at its Eleventh Plenum in April 1931.[15]

The rechristening came at the Party's First Plenum (October 1930), at which Party representatives also formally elected Tran Phu and the nine-man Central Committee and added detail to earlier instructions by accepting Tran Phu's "Political program" (Luan cuong chinh tri). The program: (a) acknowledged that the Vietnamese and world revolutions were a seamless web; (b) accepted the two-stage revolutionary scenario for Vietnam; (c) fixed as the Party's two chief tasks ending imperialism and ending feudalism in Vietnam, to be accomplished so as to skip one of the Marxist stages of development—the capitalist stage; (d) broadened the revolutionary base to root the struggle in a worker-peasant alliance. As to intra-Party matters, the Party determined:

> The essential conditions for assuring the victory of the revolution is to have a Communist Party, to use Marxism-Leninism as the ideological foundation, to have the correct political line for leading the revolution, to organize in accordance with democratic centralism, to have strict discipline, to maintain close contact with the masses, and to mature in the process of revolutionary struggle.[16]

The plenum also addressed itself to the membership problem. There had been considerable fall-away in the summer after unification. A recruitment drive was ordered, with specific instructions to concentrate on proletarians and particularly on factory workers.

ASSESSMENT OF THE INITIAL YEARS

A few conclusions and judgments can be offered about the Vietnamese proto-communist movement of the 1920s.

* It had, for a variety of reasons, a breadth of vision and because of this was able to create a first-generation, sophisticated revolutionary organization, one that appealed to the most promising Vietnamese youths but was so structured as effectively to hold its members in line.

* It had the services of Ho Chi Minh—not only his organizational genius, but also the guidance, assistance, and experience he could summon in the international fraternity of revolutionaries. This was an invaluable connection, which by comparison made indigenous revolutionary movements seem parochial and naïve.

* Relative to earlier groups, it was unified, solid in structure, and resilient and was able to reduce, at least at its core, the most serious internal weakness of revolutionary movements: meandering, argumentative disunity.

* Its day-to-day activities were based on mass action and intensive agitprop work among the proletariat, which—whatever the effect or lack of it on the ordinary Vietnamese worker—was of enormous benefit to the cadre and Party members involved, for it provided both purpose and experience.

* It had a corps of dedicated revolutionaires, carefully recruited, well trained, skillfully led, and lacking only practical experience that time alone could produce.

* It had international support, from the Comintern and from China. The importance of this can easily be exaggerated, for communism in Indochina in the 1920s was no well-ordered operation run from Moscow or Canton. In fact, it seemed at times as if the Comintern in particular had no real interest in what was happening in Indochina. Yet the movement did receive aid, both material and psychological, from both sources and without it could have died before taking root.

* Events of the 1920s largely shaped the direction the Party would take in the decade that followed. It began to shift from a bourgeois alliance to a more orthodox Marxist relationship with the proletariat, not yet having grasped the full meaning of rooting a revolution in the peasantry, although glimmerings of this notion already were clear by 1930. Proselyting of intellectuals began in earnest, along with the necessary dissembling of Party lines in order to appeal to diverse elements. Experimentation with the techniques of the united front were well under way. Finally, stress began to be placed on the idea that the Vietnamese revolution, to succeed, could not depend on the Chinese or on any other outside source of support (even though such support would in fact be necessary).

Chapter 2

The 1930s: Challenge and Frustration

The decade of the 1930s witnessed a false start for the newly formed Indochinese Communist Party in search of revolution, one that left its members in and out of the country beleaguered, disheartened and, according to the official history, "suffering courageously through a dark period of revolutionary ebb tide."[1]

The scene was indeed grim. The Party had been exposed and decimated by the French police. The apparatus was in shreds, its members in dangerous isolation. A deadly struggle had developed with the Nationalists, with control of the Vietnamese revolutionary movement as the prize. It was a battle that could have but one survivor. Serious internal division—partly doctrinal and partly organizational—had broken out as a result of the emergent competition between two brands of communism, Stalinism and Trotskyism. Finally, new imperatives of behavior and loyalty were being placed on Party members by the rise of fascism in Europe. Each of the factors impinged on the others. It is a difficult period for historians to write about, for there are, one suspects, more fictions here in the 1930s than in the entire fiction-ridden history of Vietnamese communism.

The context of the times was what was called the Great Depression, and this worldwide economic devastation took a heavy toll in Indochina. World commodity prices dropped precipitously for products the colonies exported; sales dwindled; markets dried up. But the colonial administration's fiscal demands continued, and taxes became more onerous than ever. Nature conspired, in three crop failures in a row, to make the poor of Indochina even poorer. Many of the inequities and imbalances of colonial capitalism, tolerable in the 1920 boom years, now became unbearable. The French attitude, both in Paris and Indochina, of laissez faire made a bad situation worse. Much of the economic trouble in the colonies lay beyond the effects of the depression, a fact the French were unable or unwilling to recognize. A typical rationalization was French writer Albert de Pouvourillive's 1933 explanation that rural poverty in Vietnam was "a function of natural laws, a fact of physical order, a phenomenon of a social order which escapes the device of human decisions." He complained that the communists took advantage of this natural order of things.[2] Disorders that developed, with and without Party assistance, reflected widespread economic grievances. Crowds sacked local tax offices, burned tax lists and records. None of these actions in itself was important, but the fact remains that the population of Indochina was being politicized by economic inequities, sowing the seeds of French destruction.

EARLY PARTY ORGANIZATION AND STRATEGY

The Party structure created in 1930 was original, innovative, durable, and one that much later could claim a large share of the credit for communism's ultimate victory. In a single burst of organizational creativity, a basic skeletal institution was built that, with minor alteration and refinement, remains unchanged to the present day. Its essence is three side-by-side but interlinked vertical organizational matrices— respectively, territorial, functional, and external. The French called them parallel inventories.

Territorial organization divided Vietnam into three regions or inter-zones, each administered by a regional Party Central Committee: Bac Bo (North, i.e., Tonkin), Trung Bo (Center, i.e., Annam), and Nam Bo (South, i.e., Cochin China). Each was divided into sharply compart-mentalized zones, each zone into provinces, each province into districts/sectors. At each level was a central committee and at the local level was the village or hamlet cell structure. This net controlled a shadow government from the inside.

Parallel to this was a functional organizational structure, existing largely at the district/city level with general policy guidance supplied by the national Party Central Committee. It bound together persons of like or common interest: workers, farmers, students/youth, women, military (clandestine elements in the army/militia), and elderly villagers. These social movements also were controlled from the inside by the Party.

Initial external Party links were to (a) the Third International, through the Comintern Far Eastern Bureau in Shanghai; (b) the Secretariat of the Pan-Pacific Syndicate Confederation, the Asian trade-union front organization; and (c) the League against Imperialism and for National Independence, another front organization, headquartered in Berlin.

From the start, Party leaders insisted on tight discipline, dedication to unity, and doctrinal purity. Serious mistakes were punished by death. Every member had one or more Party names. Blood oaths were administered. Information was supplied on a need-to-know basis. There was a great deal of disinformational activity. Secret society techniques (and mystique) were employed widely at the basic level.

Intertwined in this organizational structure was the Party grand strategy. International connections supported Comintern goals of the moment and augmented the work of various international front organizations. Functional organizations linked individual complaints to Party goals, one reinforcing the other. The focus was on economic grievances, colonial regime abuse, affronts to Vietnamese nationalism, plus any target opportunely to appear.

Beneath, the Party sought more fundamental objectives. Beyond liberation of Vietnam from the French was creation of a society with new social, economic, and political institutions. This objective, from the start, was never hidden, although it was only infrequently stated in public. For example, the Party stood for higher wages for workers, but only until Party control was achieved would it advocate higher standards of living made possible by greater individual income; later, it made clear, other factors than a higher standard of living would determine economic decisions. Similarly, the Party stood for distribution of land to the landless, but only for an interim period, after which all land would be collectivized. These and other doctrines were clearly enunciated even in the earliest days. The Party line was there for each to know if he cared to make the effort to examine major Party resolutions and pronouncements by top officials. The Party said what it stood for rather clearly; some elements were persistently advertised, others were stated but not frequently repeated. This can be described as lack of candor but not as hypocrisy. Dissembling would come later. At worst, the Vietnamese Communists can be charged with taking advantage of the credulity of local Vietnamese and of outsiders' will to believe.

Party strategy might have been firmly fixed, but tactics—the stuff by which strategy is implemented—largely were undifferentiated. Organization functioned smoothly, but program techniques were crude. Operational uncertainty existed in all directions. The Party leaders had not defined *enemy* clearly in their own minds: was it system or individual, French or Vietnamese, some Vietnamese or none? Should the attack be directed primarily against the imperialist (French *colon*), the feudalist (emperor and court), or the Vietnamese bourgeoisie (landlord, gentry, businessmen associated with French enterprise)? Should these enemies be attacked together or separately, in sequence or in some combination? What should be the rules of temporary alliance? Such questions probably were answerable only through experience. Revolutions grow out of peculiar local sociopolitical conditions. Each is one of a kind, and there are few universals that can be imported. The best guide becomes trial and error. Such was the case with the early Vietnamese Communists, and the cost of the lessons came high. Lack of tactical skill proved to be the main reason for the Party's first defeat, the worst it would ever suffer.

EXPERIMENT IN VIOLENCE

Having properly organized itself and settled some of its problems stemming from personality clashes, and having arranged for a systematic source of financial support, the ICP early in 1930 decided to make a quantum jump in revolutionary activity. It launched what later was officially termed a high wave of armed struggle, that is, violent militancy pressed with a vengeful passion. There were several reasons for the decision.

* The Great Depression, it was believed, had created grave economic difficulties for Indochina, making radical operations easier and more promising.

* The Party, in its inactivity, was being embarrassed by the Nationalists with their extensive militant initiatives.

* A restless impatience had developed among many young ICP cadres, some of astounding talent and energy, who had concluded that colonialism was in the process of self-destruction and that they must hurry to push that which was toppling. Also, they possessed overwhelming confidence in themselves and in Party prowess. This, in turn, created among many the fear that they were trailing behind, a cardinal sin in communist leadership.

* Comintern orders called for a *putsch* throughout Asia to undermine France, Britain, and the Netherlands. The depression was seen by many communists around the world as the arriving apocalypse, a view not shared by all Vietnamese Communists.

The time of violence for the ICP began in early 1930. By the end of the year it was over, and the Party lay in ruins. May and June saw enormous unrest develop in Indochina, taking the form of strikes, mass meetings, demonstrations, and, finally, local insurrections. Greatest activity was in the cities, particularly Vinh. The deepest struggles came in Ha Tinh and Nghe An provinces, where whole sections were in open rebellion by June. The Communists often worked alongside (but not with) the Nationalists, although in many cases it is impossible to sort out Communist-inspired violence from that staged by the Nationalists. Later, the Party claimed 129 strikes and 535 mass demonstrations during the year, a level of activity ten times greater than anything previously seen.[3] The basic ICP tactic was to trigger numerous scattered acts of political unrest that, it was hoped, would grow until they culminated in a nationwide uprising. Presumably this would begin in Tonkin, then spread to Annam, Cochin China, Cambodia, and Laos. The grand strategy, then, was piecemeal destruction of the French colonial empire in Indochina.

Late in the summer of 1930 came an attempted power seizure, the so-called Red Soviet period in which Party-encouraged villagers physically displaced local French colonial governments and established their own administrative councils, or *soviets*. Mainly, these appeared in Nghe An and Ha Tinh provinces, hence the name in official DRV history—the Nghe Tinh Soviet movement.[4] This represented a bold venture, but one in harmony with the desperate mood of the population faced with what appeared to be an ever-worsening economic situation. As a movement, it lasted about three months, although some *soviets* were still in existence a year later, the French finding them more difficult to eradicate than anticipated. The *soviets* seized large land holdings and redistributed them. They sought to effect major change in local social and educational institutions. They were authentically revolutionary: "The *Soviets* repressed anti-revolutionaries, gave democratic freedoms, distributed land, encouraged learning and discarded superstition."[5]

Throughout, there was considerable violence, some of it apparently beyond cadre control. Landlords were drowned, local village officials hanged. Much of the terror was directed against Vietnamese collaborators rather than the French *colon*. This was a double error, as the Party later recognized. It divided Vietnamese at a moment when unity was called for. It created the wrong enemy, the local Vietnamese official—more victim than villain, whose removal in any case would not appreciably advance the Party cause—rather than the colonial system.

The Central Committee (and the Comintern itself) viewed some *soviet* activity with marked displeasure. The attack on religion ("discarding superstititon") was deemed premature. Many of the killings were nothing more than murder behind an ideological facade, and the Comintern was moved to declare that such violence was not consonant with the "proper organized violence" called for in Marxist doctrine.[6] Some ICP leaders, including Ho Chi Minh, were distinctly cool to village terrorism. Indeed, many Vietnamese believe that Ho from the start had been against the entire period of violence.

As often happens in attempts at revolutionary change, excesses were committed that played into the hands of the worst elements of the incumbent, the reactionaries. Official French *colon* response—against communist and nationalist alike—was swift, total, and untempered by previously exercised restraints. Villages were shelled and strafed. Mass roundups of villagers ended in summary execution for hundreds, with others sent to the guillotine after quick trial. Some 10,000 Vietnamese (and two French) died during the year, about 100,000 were jailed, and another 50,000 exiled to remote French colonies in the South Seas and Africa.[7]

The Party suffered grievously during the White Terror, as official history now terms it. Much of the ICP apparat was laid bare, the payoff of careful French penetration efforts and extensive betrayal. Fear and panic among cadre and rank and file bred more betrayal. In the end, virtually the entire Party Central Committee had been sold out by fellow communists. ICP Secretary General Tran Phu was jailed and died in prison, reportedly tortured to death. Nearly all ICP cadres not arrested fled the country. The Nationalists suffered in like fashion: 10,000 members received jail sentences, 13 Viet Nam Quoc Dan Dang (VNQDD) leaders were guillotined, and the movement was decimated. French courts tried many of the *soviet* members, chiefly on criminal charges. Here the axe fell on collaborators and dupes, because most Party members wisely had kept free of criminal activity and thus received only house arrest sentences or short periods of detention. Ho Chi Minh remained out of the country during this time, but even so did not escape. While in Hong Kong for the Party's Second Plenum in October 1930, he was arrested by the British, on French request, and imprisoned for some two years.[8]

While this audacious experiment in violence was devastating to Party personnel and organization, some grim advantage came of it. The Nationalist movement was ruined, having suffered a proportionately greater loss than the Communist, and never again would have the advantage it enjoyed previously. The experiment also was enormously useful for future agitprop cadres. The year 1930 became the high point in historical heroism. Legends were born in the midst of hopeless combat, spirit forged by the fires of glorious defeat. It was a time of myth building, one on which the Party has traded ever since. Finally, the experiment was of tremendous educative value for those Party cadre and members who managed to survive it. Human considerations aside, the 1930 lesson in the practice of armed struggle probably should be put down as a plus, not a minus. Not for the last time would the Vietnamese Communists gain through audacity what they lost through tactical error.

In organizational terms, however, the Party in mid-1932 was at the lowest point it would ever reach in its history. As a revolutionary movement it had been rendered temporarily impotent. What remained was Ho Chi Minh and a small cadre corps, still unshaken in faith, still as determined as ever. To the outside world, the ICP was moribund. Inside, quietly and secretly, it was being rebuilt and reenergized.

The first reconstruction efforts ended in a second failure—again the Party was penetrated by police agents, aided once more by informants and traitors, and once again destroyed as a functioning unit. Then, in 1933, came the second reconstruction, this time carefully and cleverly advised by Comintern experts and managed by some of the most valuable cadres, who had fled early and now were smuggled back into Vietnam as supervisors. Rebuilding was done in deepest secrecy with

enormous attention paid to internal security. A new image was projected. The Party made itself reasonable, pursuing what was called the
legal struggle route[9] and seeking cooperation with moderate elements
both in Indochina and in France. It launched what was to become a
systematic, generation-long campaign of throwing sand in the eyes of
the world, confusing outsiders as to exactly how extremist the movement
was. Inside and outside the Party the word spread: zeal no longer was in
fashion; fears of the Party must be allayed. This legal struggle phase, a
campaign of calculated blandness, had almost immediate effect in
reducing police pressure and making new friends in Paris.

Still, for most of the remainder of the decade the ICP was a limping
operation. The best cadres were still in prison or deeply hidden. Party
funds were scarce. Liaison and communication networks were only
slowly rebuilt. Regionalism, with its attendant suspicion and cross purpose, continued to increase.

Only from the South was progress reported. There, developmental
work went ahead under the guidance of Tran Van Giau, who in October
1932, had arrived back in Saigon from Moscow training. In 1933 he re-
established the Cochin China Region Central Committee (headquartered in Hau Giang province) and vested it with extraordinary authority.
He reconstituted an old front organization—as the League against Imperialism, with a nonviolent charter, and sought centrist support. All
acts of terror were officially halted. New publishing ventures were
launched. A courier system employing Vietnamese sailors on merchant
ships was established. Giau concentrated on the problem areas: training
cadres (those in jail were the best students, just as prisons were the best
schools for revolutionaries), developing sources of revenue (including
bank robbery), quieting the fears of his enemies, and, above all, creating
an organization that could withstand any attack. During this time new
figures were moving to the front of the movement, including Ha Huy
Tap, Phung Chi Kien, and, most prominently, Le Hong Phong. In 1934,
the latter was named to head the Comintern's new control instrument
for Vietnam, the Overseas Section (or Leadership Committee) headquartered in Macao. This five-to-seven-man group ran the Party in
Indochina through a series of regional committees, published an important theoretical journal called *Bolshevik,* and staged several conferences, including the First Party Congress.

Only ten persons attended the First Party Congress, held in Macao

March 27–31, 1935. Out of the gathering came amended Party and Youth League bylaws, reorganization of the four major front organizations (Peasant's Association, Antiimperialist League, Red Relief Association, and Indochinese General Federation of Labor), a new political resolution, and a manifesto. The sense of the policy statements was the conclusion that mass disorders, civil disobedience, and other forms of low-grade resistance would not drive out the French. What was required, said the congress, was "conditioning"—preparation for a general uprising (or revolution),[10] including meticulous organizational work as part of the preparation—meanwhile awaiting what was called the correct circumstance, that is, some great social upheaval that would provide the opportunity needed (for example, what World War I was for the Bolsheviks in Russia). Later histories also claimed that the congress anticipated the united-front stop-Hitler movement, since that was one of the three tasks set down by the congress. Specifically, these were: (1) build the Party and organizational strength (the intent here was in part directed against the Trotskyists), (2) broaden the base of the Party's appeal, and (3) oppose imperialist war.

The Party grew during the period after the congress. This was due chiefly to its united-front approach.[11] Exact figures are not available, but one Party history says that membership at the time of the First Congress totaled "in the hundreds," adding that it increased by 60 percent between early 1936 and late 1937. By this time the Party essentially had been reconstituted.

THE NATIONALIST CHALLENGE

The radical Vietnamese attack on French colonialism, from its inception in the late 1920s, had locked in bitter and deadly embrace two great matrices of revolution, the Communists and the Nationalists. Basically, it was a battle for a monopoly of political power; it was fought with the knowledge on both sides that, whatever short-run alliances might be arranged, in the end there would be only one winner, one survivor. Vietnam's political history during the past fifty years very largely can be written in terms of this struggle.

The Nationalist movement, as the term is used here, was that cluster of organizations which sought emancipation from the French and rejected both reformism (in favor of ultramilitancy) and communism. Its quarrel with communism was based on communism's doctrinal trappings and on its estimate that communism served alien interests more than it served those of Vietnam. This is not to imply that the Vietnamese Communists were not nationalist. The ICP and its successor organizations embraced the abstraction known as nationalism—as have all twentieth-century Vietnamese political movements. Use of the term here is technical and grows out of Vietnamese history and the labels employed by the Vietnamese in the past half century. Vietnamese usage, but not Vietnamese perception, has been that in the anticolonial struggle the Nationalists were on one side and on the other was their opposition—over the years, variously called Communist, Viet Minh, National Liberation Front, Viet Cong, and other names. As late as the early 1960s, the author, interviewing older villagers in South Vietnam, was obliged to use only two terms, Nationalist (to mean the Government of Vietnam, or GVN, forces) and Viet Minh (to mean the National Liberation Front, or Viet Cong.) Other terms led to confusion or lack of comprehension. The genesis of this usage apparently lies in the imprecise nature of ideological positions in the pre-1930 period, when few could or did distinguish between Marxist and non-Marxist revolution. Some individuals, it is true, saw themselves as communists or noncommunists or even anticommunists, but few had a fully articulated ideology or even a clearly formulated belief system. The doctrinal position of the Thanh Nien—modern-day Vietnamese communism's closest ancestor—was highly impure communism by later standards. On the other hand, many opponents of the Thanh Nien embraced Marxist thought to a surprising extent. This is a phenomenon that Frank Trager has termed the communist-nationalist amalgam. Radicals were clearly radical and all stood for revolution, but their ideological systems were primitive, amorphous, and overlapping. What counted most in the early days were personality, geographic regionalism, organizational heritage, education, and social experience. These, rather than ideology, largely distinguished one revolutionary from another. Not until the mid-1930s, when genuine doctrinal confrontation developed—Nationalist versus Communist as well as Stalinist versus Trotskyist—were revolutionaries forced to think through exactly what they did and did not believe.

The Nationalist movement, which developed in Vietnam's politically turbulent late twenties and early thirties, comprised a vast and bewildering welter of individual organizations. More than 100 organizational names can be found (often varying by a single adjective) in records and literature of the era. Statistically, they averaged perhaps fifty persons per organization. The mortality rate of the groups was high, but there was great continuity in personnel as individuals moved from one to another. Organizations were created, disbanded, reformed, dissolved, and reunited in kaleidoscopic profusion. The Surete set up its own Nationalist organizations for purposes of entrapment. There were organizations within organizations, single facades hiding clusters of groups, fronts behind which there was nothing. Leaders lied about their membership strength, their political purpose, their willingness to make alliances, their outside connections. Organization was pitted against organization in a great game of political intrigue in which tactics of proselytism, penetration, espionage, sabotage, and betrayal to the police were used freely. Some groups existed simply to traffic in the appeal of the secret society while purporting to be politically militant. A group significant in one part of Vietnam was unknown elsewhere. Some organizations were mere personal vehicles, consisting of no more than a leader, an imposing title, and a few friends who met afternoons at a Saigon sidewalk cafe to discuss politics. Many were not political parties nor political organizations at all, but only—as the French exquisitely expressed it—political tendencies.

This description is not set forth to deprecate the Vietnamese Nationalist movement, which was genuine, serious, and possibly could have become the ruling force in today's Vietnam. Rather, it is to indicate that the movement operated in a sociopolitical environment that was part fantasy and to suggest the existence of an irrational dimension that always must be borne in mind.

The authentic Vietnamese Nationalist organizational streams—or, more correctly, the several thousand Nationalists who joined and stayed with the movement through the years—flowed from four sources that, for the sake of simplicity, can be labeled Chinese, Japanese, indigenous, and religious.

The first, oldest, and most important stream of Nationalist organizations was that modeled after, and often supported by, the Chinese Nationalists, or the KMT. The leading group here, and the only one to survive the 1920s, was the Viet Nam Quoc Dan Dang (VNQDD), often called simply the QDD. It was founded in 1927 by Nguyen Thai Hoc, a twenty-three-year old Hanoi primary-school teacher, and his brother, who ran a printing house in Hanoi called the Annamese Library. The latter provided the revenue and the legal facade behind which the VNQDD initially operated. Its spiritual lineage can be traced back roughly to Phan Boi Chau, one of the earliest and most revered figures in modern Vietnamese Nationalist history. While detailed consideration of the VNQDD is beyond the scope of this book, certain characteristics are relevant to our interest.

The VNQDD was patterned after the KMT organization and embraced Sun Yat-sen's "doctrine of the three people"—that is, sovereignty, family, and welfare, or, roughly, democracy, nationalism, and socialism. It saw itself as traditionally Vietnamese, rooted in the village gentry, if not peasantry. Its leadership came more or less equally from four social elements: the colonial government, the educational system, the armed forces and militia, and commercial enterprises. Rank-and-file members were chiefly students, with scatterings of small businessmen, civil servants, and ethnic Vietnamese members of the French army. While this composition appears to be bourgeois, the VNQDD was in fact more proletarian than its Communist rival of the 1920s. While few VNQDD came from the lowest end of the social spectrum, neither were there rich merchants, big landowners, or famous scholars. The early Communist movement contained many sons of mandarins, large estate owners, and the well-to-do, attracted not by proletarian appeals (the VNQDD approach) but by the "scientific nature" of communism. The VNQDD clearly had appeal and by mid-1929 had built a 120-cell, 1,500-member organization in the central Tonkin region. It borrowed heavily from communist organizational structure; it was centralist, vanguard, and cellular. It was Tonkin-centered, proletarian-oriented in theory, and divided its activities into the triad of legal, semilegal, and illegal. Much of its language was Marxist, perhaps the result of Marxist influence among French *colon* teachers who had provided the early education of many VNQDD as well as ICP cadres and members. In many ways, the VNQDD was communist in all but name and in loyalty to a foreign communist center.[12]

From its earliest days, the VNQDD was bloody-handed, even more so perhaps than were the Communists. In early 1929 its members attempted to assassinate a French governor general and did succeed in killing his associate, M. Bazin, chief of the infamous French colonial labor service that dragooned Vietnamese laborers into duty on French plantations throughout the empire. In February 1930 it staged the most ambitious anti-French effort in Vietnam to that date, the famed Yen Bay uprising, a badly bungled mutiny by Vietnamese soldiers serving in the French army. Nguyen Thai Hoc was captured and executed along with twelve members of his central committee and several hundred members. Most of the leaders fled to China.[13]

Always and everywhere, the VNQDD was rent by the twin curses of Vietnamese revolutionary movements—personality clash and geographic regionalism. Doctrinal differences did exist within the movement but were of secondary importance. The central struggle, within and outside the VNQDD, was the struggle for power, for control. While it flirted with liaisons and common fronts with the Communists (and, earlier, with the Tan Viet) these never came to much. Ho Chi Minh tried without success to establish a united front with the VNQDD in the late 1920s, an effort he would return to a decade later. While alliances might be useful, neither Ho nor the ICP ever entertained any illusions about the VNQDD. It was regarded as genuinely antiimperialist but only at a bourgeois revolutionary level; it was viewed much as the Bolsheviks saw their arch-rivals, the Mensheviks, that is, as a movement dedicated only to ending the existing ruling system, not to the complete restructuring of the social order. The ICP did learn from its early rival, though, such things as techniques for proselyting among Vietnamese in the French army, an activity pioneered by the VNQDD.

The second major Vietnamese Nationalist stream traced its spiritual home to pre-war Japan. The main element here was commonly called the Dai Viet (or Greater Vietnam) movement, *dai* meaning "great" in Vietnamese and Japanese (and Chinese).

Excesses by Japan's Imperial Army during World War II as well as the total discrediting of Japan's military governments of the 1930s have, in postwar years, tended to obscure the fact that for a time Japan was enormously attractive to many Vietnamese revolutionaries. Here was an Asian country that had escaped colonialism, even escaped the imperialist restrictions that had humiliated China; that had defeated a European power, Russia, in a modern war; and that stood as an alternative to the cultural imperialism of the West. Further, with its call for "Asia for the Asiatics" and under the banner of its Co-Prosperity Sphere, Japan for a time offered its support to those who resisted colonialism. It was easy for many in Asia, then, to deny what later became evident, that the Co-Prosperity Sphere was just another name for Japanese imperialism.

The stream of Vietnamese Nationalism associated with Japan began with Prince Cuong De, pretender to the Annam throne, who had lived in Japan since World War I. The group that supported return of the prince was called the Vietnam Phuc Quoc Dong Minh Hoi (Vietnam Restoration Association), or, usually, the Phuc Quoc.[14] In Vietnam, during the initial period, most revolutionaries with an affinity for Japan were part of a vague structure—more notion than organization—called the Dong Du, or Eastward Movement.[15] Its greatest strength perhaps came as a residue of negatives; young revolutionaries, looking for a spiritual home and rejecting China for ethnic reasons and France for cultural reasons, settled on Japan as the least worse compromise.

The Dai Viet was an authoritarian, elitist movement that rejected the mass-base approach of the Communists. Its politics were monarchist, its economics socialist. It possessed a high level of coup d'etat mentality. It became, much later and briefly, a major political force in Vietnam. During the 1930s most revolutionaries with an affinity for Japan worked in the ranks of the VNQDD; in fact, the first Dai Viet organization, the Dai Viet Quoc Dan Dang (Greater Vietnam Nationalist Party), was a VNQDD breakaway group, one that was formed in 1939 by Truong Tu Anh (killed in 1945 by the Communists). Dai Viet members included Vietnamese scholars and colonial government officials, many of whom had been educated in Japan. The Dai Viet as a Nationalist movement flourished, obviously, during World War II, when its mentor occupied Indochina. Equally obvious is the fact that, when the Japanese departed, most of the Dai Viet political strength went with them. As late as the 1950s, however, the Dai Viets were claiming a strength of 200,000, most of it concentrated in northern South Vietnam, in the provinces of Quang Tri, Quang Nam, and Thua Thien.[16]

The third stream of Nationalist organizations is termed here, for want of a better expression, the indigenous stream (which is not meant to imply that the others were nonindigenous). It comprised those generally ill-fated movements with no particular outside material or spiritual support, peopled mostly by small groups of youths moved by idealism and revolutionary zeal.

Foremost of these was the Tan Viet Cach Mang Dang, or Tan Viet (often Giai Huan). It was founded by Le Van Huan, Vo Hoanh, and Hoang Van Khai and was the first, and for a time only, interior Vietnam revolutionary group, others being Canton-based. Its membership, numbering around 1,000 and divided into five-man cells, was almost entirely middle-class intellectual, officially avoiding the proletariat. It was a mixture of reformism and, later, revolution. In some ways, the Tan Viet was a bridge between the two eras of Phan Boi Chau and Ho Chi Minh. It had no clearly formulated doctrine nor course of political action, and it offered a wordy but vaguely articulated quasi-Marxist philosophy. Today, it probably would be labeled a national communist or Titoist movement. It strongly advocated Vietnamese revolutionary separation from the influences of the KMT and Moscow. It stood for "moral, intellectual, and economic revival of Vietnam under a republican government" as early Tan Viet statements put it, but it incorporated many of the ideas of Karl Marx. "Pick and choose communism" was a later contemptuous description by Hanoi historians.

In 1930 the Tan Viet was betrayed in an ICP intelligence operation that supplied the Surete with the information needed to destroy it. Most surviving members moved to the ICP or the VNQDD.

Duy Dao Anh was secretary general of the Tan Viet and author of the first original communist writing by a Vietnamese (*Study of the Vietnam revolution,* circa mid-1920s), which put forth the idea of Vietnamese Communists as nationalists first and proletarian internationalists second and which supposedly had considerable influence on Ho Chi Minh's thinking. Anh betrayed the Tan Viet in 1930 by selling its membership list to the French. He switched loyalties to the Communists, but they never trusted him and he held only minor posts until his death in Hanoi in 1960.

A second element in the indigenous stream was the Nguyen An Ninh Youth Association (1927–30), named for and by its journalist founder, who created it upon his return from France as a bitter Francophobe. It operated in Cochin China under the secret name of Cao Vong Thanh Nien Dang, or Hope of Youth Party. Agrarian-socialist in doctrine, cellular in organization, it allied its 800 some members with the gentry and with politically awakened rural Vietnamese. Ninh was betrayed and arrested in 1929, and most of the movement's members gravitated to the Thanh Nien and then to the ICP. It is remembered today for Ninh's underground newspaper, which made some of the most trenchant and scathing attacks on French colonialism ever penned by a Vietnamese.

Other groups of this stream: the Quang Phuc Hoi, a collection of secret societies in Annam high schools and predecessor of the Tan Viet; also the Viet Nam Doc Lap Doan or Viet Doan, a collection of one-man political coteries.

While most of these indigenous Nationalist organizations died early, their members continued active, working either in or out of other Nationalist groups. The structure was gone, but influence remained.

The fourth and final stream of Nationalist movements was the sacred-based, mainly the two famed Vietnamese sects, Cao Dai and Hoa Hao, but also, later and in a different context, the Buddhist and Roman Catholic religions.

The Vietnamese sect was what sociologists call an undifferentiated social movement, that is, one concerned with all aspects of a member's life—economic, political, social, spiritual—from the cradle to the grave. To outsiders, the sect was a combination pro-Nationalist group, militant religious order, and traditionalist social movement advocating a return to the old ways.

The Cao Dai, formed by Ngo Van Chieu in 1919 (formally organized in 1925) was, or became, a crypto-political movement, ostensibly a religious order, but one conducting political activity beneath several layers of secret societies, the most important being Pham Mon. Cao Daism was a genuine, if somewhat strange, religion. Its theme was spiritual synthesis: that all major religious figures—Christ, Muhammad, Buddha, even Confucius—were separate incarnations of the same being and thus that all religions are one. It stood for a traditionalist social structure, hierarchical, ordered, unchanging. Since it wanted to move society backward, not to some utopian future, French presence represented less of a problem; and the Cao Dai, though nationalist from the earliest days, was less anti-French than were other movements.

Because of its clever clandestinism, it still is not clear when Cao Dai political activism began. Apparently, it was nonpolitical in its early years, a condition that changed in the mid-1920s. The Surete was astounded at the number of Cao Dai political infiltrators uncovered in its great 1930 exposé of Vietnamese revolutionaries. The sect was politically quiescent during the 1930s, becoming active again in 1943 with the formation of its more or less open political arm, the Vietnam Restoration Association. It soon split (as did the church itself) into two factions. The Cao Dai had a relationship, never satisfactorily explained, with the old Phuc Quoc (Prince Cuong De's monarchist group) and with the Dai Viets, a relationship that resulted in something of a pro-Japanese attitude. It had a good working connection with the Japanese during World War II. It collaborated with the Viet Minh during the war against the French, although never too closely, then opposed the new government of Ngo Dinh Diem but cooperated with Diem's successors.

The Hoa Hao was formed in 1939 by a southern mystic and faith healer, Huynh Phu So. According to legend, he was sent to a lunatic asylum, where he converted his psychiatrist. This organization too was crypto-Nationalist, its political arm finally surfacing late in World War II as the Dan Xa Social Democratic Party (which later factionalized). Hoa Hao priests preached a vague message of independence from the French and traditionalist social reform, quoting as their authority obscure ancient texts and prophecies. The French interned So in 1941. He was released by the Japanese, and he and his organization appeared to collaborate closely with the Japanese occupation forces, although it was apparent later that this was a double game and that the Hoa Hao throughout the war had been consistently and secretly anti-Japanese.

Both the Cao Dai and Hoa Hao sects were geographically located in the South, the Cao Dai chiefly in Tay Ninh province and the Hoa Hao in An Giang province. While never trusting the Communists, they were at times willing to collaborate with them; but given their bastion-like position, they tended more to take a live-and-let-live attitude toward other radicals. Some sect assertions and performance may have been strategy. A religious movement preaching return to traditional values would appear to the French as the virtual opposite of a revolutionary group with outside support. It is clear in retrospect that sect behavior in part consisted of the deliberate and successful pursuit of nationalist goals—and the communication of this to followers—behind a religious screen, but to what degree this pursuit represented the raison d'être of the sect still is impossible to determine. Surveying sect history leaves one with a deep respect for the ability and masterfulness of sect leaders. They were in every way equal in cleverness—or deviousness—to other Nationalist and Communist leaders. If anything, they were superior in devising an anticolonial strategy that had built into it protection against the kind of total decimation suffered by both Communist and Nationalist groups. Had the sects been forward-facing rather than backward-turning, the history of the Vietnamese revolution might have been quite different.

Nationalism played a role in both Buddhist and Roman Catholic affairs from the 1920s onward. Both were sympathetic to the anticolonial movement, and neither viewed the Communist movement with the degree of apprehension common elsewhere.

Vietnamese Buddhism began early to divide into what became two great doctrinal movements involving social change, the so-called quiescent

Buddhists and the activist Buddhists. The first took an other-world view, holding that since nothing in this world is ultimately important nothing can be immediately important; therefore, no worldly activity, including politics, has any significance. The only purpose of this life is to get through it properly and be reborn to a higher order; Buddhists in politics should engage as secular individuals, not as Buddhists. This view was opposed by those who believed that Buddhism does and must contain elements of social responsibility, that the condition of man here and now is relevant to Buddhist belief and behavior; therefore, it is imperative that Buddhism as an idea and Buddhists as individuals be an integral part of political activity.

Throughout Vietnam, and throughout Asia, this debate has raged for decades, although in each Asian country the tendency is for one faction to become dominant. Thus, we have on the one hand Thailand or Burma, examples of quiescent Buddhism, and on the other Sri Lanka, where (when it was still Ceylon) a Buddhist priest assassinated the prime minister. In Vietnam, the ratio was about three to two in favor of quiescence, but gradually shifting over the years toward activism.

Throughout the early years there were nationalist stirrings in many temples. Buddhism is not sharply hierarchical, nor is there much organizational superstructure above the pagoda level; hence individual temples enjoy considerable latitude in deciding on political activity. During the 1930s, most Buddhist temples supported the Nationalist movement to some degree, offering food and shelter and, most importantly, secret sanctuary to revolutionaries. Nationalist sentiment grew steadily among young monks. Buddhist treatment of communism tended to be contemptuous in intellectual terms, especially in the Hue area. Communist ideology was dismissed as a shallow, pretentious newcomer to the world of ideas, in no way comparable to the soaring thought of Buddhism, which had developed through twenty-five centuries.

Most Vietnamese Catholics of the period were pro-French. Some young Catholics became involved in progressive activity, but Catholic sentiment always was nationalist rather than revolutionary in that it stood for emancipation from colonialism but not revolutionary change of social institutions. The kind of Catholic radicalism that developed in South America, for example, never was present in Vietnam.

In both instances, then—Buddhism and Catholicism—religion did not provide much support for the early Communist movement, but neither did it represent any sort of a major barrier to its advancement.

TROTSKYISM AND THE DEMOCRATIC FRONT

Life in Vietnam in the later 1930s was outwardly tranquil. Economic recovery had removed the worst of the earlier strain, and a new liberal government in Paris gave promise of political concession in the colonies. Some of the initial lure of revolution among the young had waned. The ICP, now reconstructed, had held its first congress (1935) and produced a program more reasonable than earlier ones. Although the Party was engaged in a deep and bitter struggle with the variant of communism called Trotskyism, this seldom broke the surface of the political sea. The late 1930s also was a time of normalization for the Party, when it became integrated into the grand strategy of international communism. This imposed on local Party members exacting behavior and had a deleterious effect in the struggle with the Trotskyists.

The First Congress fixed a new policy on colonialism. Previously the Party had held for separation of the colonies from the mother country, that is, the outright emancipation of Indochina. The new line was the right of self-determination, with collaboration or not as one chose—a policy far more benign as far as the metropolitan French, or even the *colon,* were concerned. Officially this was described:

> The main task of the Party is to concentrate efforts, and not try to do everything at the same time, for this only leads to unsatisfactory results. The Congress therefore asks all Party organizations to concentrate on these three main tasks: (a) Consolidate and develop Party organization; (b) Increase support by the proletariat; (c) Struggle against entering into a war among imperialists.[17]

The Congress also moved the ICP Central Committee headquarters to the politically softer South. There, more so than in the Center and North, it began to experiment with newly emerging political possibilities made possible by the united front.

In the next five years the Party grew in size, strength, influence, and sense of certitude. It engaged in considerable agitprop work, made possible by increased French permissiveness. At one point it was publishing some thirty periodicals (many of them local or regional) on a regular basis. Compartmentalization of the Party into legal, semi-legal, and illegal activities was refined and developed. The Popular Front, organized in May 1936 on Comintern orders, flourished, eventually consisting of an estimated 1,500 subgroups, most of them small action units as they were called. This, and the working alliance with the French Socialist Party, constituted the major legal activity. Semilegal activity consisted of strikes and labor stoppages (the Party claimed responsibility for 640 strikes in the eighteen months from mid-1936 to late 1937); school boycotts; publicly staged mock trials called taking the floor; and, of course, the ubiquitous public demonstration, large and small. May Day 1938 was the high point in this effort. In Hanoi a giant rally was staged, involving some 50,000 persons, including hundreds of ICP members (some under the Socialist banner).

Instances of illegal activity during the period followed the customary pattern of espionage, sabotage, and assassination.

For all Communists, in and out of Vietnam, the second half of the 1930s was dominated by the rise of Fascism in Europe and the Party's stop-Hitler movement, launched as the Popular or Democratic Front. This strategy sought to unite in one large organization all other organizations, Communist and non-Communist alike, which could agree to submerge their differences for the common purpose of meeting the Fascist threat.

The Democratic Front began with the Comintern's Seventh Congress in the summer of 1935 and ended four years later at the November 1939 plenum, which declared that the Democratic Front strategy no longer was appropriate. Officially, the period in Vietnam is recorded thus:

In July 1935 the Communist International held its Seventh Congress in Moscow. In its resolution as well as in Dimitrov's report to the Congress, the Communist International assessed that the most dangerous immediate enemy of the world's people was not imperialism in general but the fascist imperialists; the task of the international working class was to unify their own ranks and found a broad front with the other classes and strata of people in order to struggle against fascism and war. . . .

In this situation, the Central Committee held a Session in July 1936, convened by Comrade Le Hong Phong. Basing itself on the resolution of the Seventh Congress of the Communist International and starting from the concrete conditions of Viet Nam at that time, the Session temporarily decided not to put forth the slogans "To defeat French imperialists" and "To requisition the landlords' land and distribute it to the peasants." It advocated the founding of the broad *Anti-Imperialist People's Front* embracing all classes, political parties, religious organizations, and nationalities in Indochina, in order to struggle together for elementary democratic rights.[18]

This was a difficult order to implement and immediately caused internal problems. Factions within the Party opposed collaboration with reform parties, opposed concentration on the use of legal and semilegal methods, or favored "unprincipled cooperation" with the Trotskyists.

The Comintern, at the time of launching the Democratic Front, also effected an internal reorganization that switched routine supervision of the ICP from the Comintern in Moscow to the French Communist Party in Paris. For a period, the ICP was virtually an appendage of the FCP, a significant development.

The meaning of the Comintern order on the front was that the ICP was required to focus on the distant danger of European Fascism rather than on the immediate inequities of French colonialism. It was forced to zig and zag, along with communist parties everywhere, to keep step with Moscow (as world communist leader) in its dealings with Hitler: first Hitler was imminent enemy, then chief ally, then enemy again. While this might have made sense to a Russian Communist, for most Indochinese militants it seemed subservient and irrelevant behavior. Protection of the USSR, at all costs, as communism's homeland was a mere abstraction.

Even more painful was the requirement that the Party lie down with the hated French *colon* overlord. Both the French Communist Party and the Comintern were firm and unrelenting on this; both insisted that the sole momentary objective was defeat of Fascism, from which nothing must detract. At the very moment French colonialism was most vulnerable the order came: don't further weaken; collaborate. Capitalism might be attacked, but not colonial administration.

All this stood in embarrassed contrast to the unwavering militancy of the Vietnamese—Communists, Nationalists, and Trotskyists alike. A revolutionary might acknowledge that the effort to stop Hitler made sense for Europe perhaps, but in Indochina it was not worth the price of a great wasted opportunity. Small wonder that Ho Chi Minh hunkered down somewhere during the 1930s—we still don't know where he spent most of that decade—for had he been in Indochina his credibility would have been stretched to the breaking point, probably ruining him.

The policy also put an obvious strain on the ICP-Comintern relationship, which in turn resulted in (and permitted) a somewhat more independent ICP line than might otherwise have been the case. For example, it enabled the ICP from time to time to work with the Trotskyists in Indochina. Vietnamese who lived through the era also say that Party-*colon* collaboration often was more apparent than real.

Within Vietnam, the division between Stalinist and Trotskyist stemmed from doctrinal debate on how best to make revolution, the same issue that divided the two factions internationally. In the ICP ranks were many latent deviationists, that is, Trotskyists, and their movement had considerable appeal, especially in the South. It was radical enough for any Vietnamese. It conveyed a straightforward image of honest revolution, the call to all-out battle against the white and yellow sharks (i.e., French *colon* and Chinese money lender), and its integrity was unsullied by orders from foreign masters to temporize the crusade.

The break in Vietnam came at the 1937 ICP plenum in Saigon, which had as its main order of business consideration of the Comintern directive to launch a local Democratic Front movement and to coordinate activities with the French Communist Party. Some in the plenum challenged these orders, calling instead for total opposition to colonialism and for worldwide permanent revolution. The issue split leaders and rank and file alike.

As an alternative to Stalinism, the Trotskyist movement in the communist world, and in communist-influenced circles, was a curiosity, even a joke, but not a serious challenge. But at the same time, it was a durable if strange phenomenon in international terms, one that engendered odd and persistent pockets of strength in Ceylon, Peru, California, and, more than anywhere else perhaps, Vietnam. Trotsky's thinking had a peculiarly seductive hold on young Vietnamese.

The Fourth International Party (the name assumed by the Trotskyist movement in the late 1930s), as well as the movement itself in Vietnam, was largely the creation of one man, Ta Thu Thau, a gifted southerner, French-educated and Moscow-trained, who arrived in Saigon in 1932 to begin organizational efforts. Originally his movement was called the Ta Thu Thau Organization. It remained a single entity through a time of troubles marked by heavy and effective French police suppression efforts and continuous internal strife over various reorganization proposals. Then it split into two competing elements. The major faction was called the Struggle Group, after its publication, *Struggle*, headed by Ta Thu Thau and his two chief lieutenants, Tran Van Thach and Phan Van Hum. It claimed an activist or cadre strength of 3,000, mostly in Cochin China. Its opposition, the October Group, regarded itself as pure Trotskyist, whereas the Struggle Group included members who considered themselves communists, but neither Stalinists nor

Trotskyists. Most of the differences between the two groups resulted from entourage politics. Doctrinal disputes turned mainly on tactical questions, such as the degree of short-run cooperation with the Stalinists.

The Trotskyist movement in Cochin China pursued, as did the ICP for a while, the legal route of the franchise, its members engaging in such election activity as the French permitted. Candidates entered the Saigon municipal elections from 1933 to 1939, running for offices that were mainly advisory, although they did have some local political importance. Ta Thu Thau was elected to the Saigon Municipal Council in 1937. In the Cochin China Council elections of 1939—Trotskyism's finest hour—Trotskyist candidates won 80 percent of the votes, against a combined field of Stalinists, Nationalists, reformists, and collaborationists. The movement was weaker in the North, where Tran Van Phuong was the only important Trotskyist figure of the 1930s.

But it was dealt a swift and sudden death blow on September 1, 1939, the day World War II began. According to reliable sources, the day the war began someone delivered to Surete headquarters in Saigon the full Fourth International Party membership roster, listing names, aliases, addresses, and locations of every Trotskyist in the country.[19] Within hours French police had rounded up virtually all leaders and dispatched them to the New Hebrides, New Caledonia, Madagascar, and other French colonies remote from Indochina. Some of them or their descendants are there to this day. That such a packet of information was delivered seems reasonably certain; from whence it came has never been established. Years later, many Vietnamese historians and political scientists in Saigon asserted that only the ICP had the resources and the capability to accomplish such a feat of tactical intelligence. The ICP regarded the Trotskyist movement with the particular hatred communists hold for their own kind deemed guilty of deviationism. Certainly the Party stood to gain the most by eliminating the Trotskyists. In any event, the movement in Vietnam was decapitated in an instant. Its remnants managed to survive World War II, the Fourth International Party again splitting—into the Struggle Group and the International Communist League—never again to merge. Gradually Trotskyism disappeared as an organized force in Vietnam. Ta Thu Thau, imprisoned by the French, was released by the Japanese near the end of the war, only to be seized by the Viet Minh and executed by firing squad.

From its earliest days, Trotskyism in Vietnam knew only enemies: the ICP, the various Nationalists, the French Communist Party, the Surete. Beset from all quarters, the movement perhaps was doomed from the start. Yet, for one brief moment, in the southern region of Vietnam, it was the dominant banner carrier of the revolution. Throughout the 1930s it had enormous appeal, especially to the young, and it left a lingering bouquet long after it had ceased to exist as a political force. Decades later—in the early 1960s—freshly printed propaganda leaflets would appear mysteriously from time to time in the Mekong Delta region, bearing anachronistic Trotskyist messages and signed by unknown organizations claiming loyalty to Leon Trotsky.

CRITIQUE OF THE NATIONALISTS VERSUS THE COMMUNISTS

The Communists in a single decade supplanted the Nationalists as the leading revolutionary force in Vietnam. There are several reasons for this:

* The political-economic scene basically favored the Communists. Vietnam did not have the nationalist tradition in politics known elsewhere in Asia, for example, in India. With the limits on political acculturation set by the French, no genuine nationalist alternative could develop. The Nationalist movement that did emerge, therefore, was warped, that is, exclusive, authoritarian, sectarian, and bloody-handed. It never could become a means of developing national leaders nor an instrument for rectification of legitimate grievance nor even a channel of public opinion on *colon* excesses. French denial of political rights played more into the hands of the Communists than into the hands of the Nationalists. The economic system in Indochina—colonial capitalism—was alien, exploitative, and of little benefit to the Indochinese, and it too served better the Communist than the Nationalist cause. Thus French politics, and French stupidity, shaped a climate in which communist strategy became the most appropriate, the most feasible, and the most attractive of all available anticolonial strategic choices. As desperation grew, nothing except communism could offer real promise of success against colonialism.

* The Nationalists were their own worst enemies. Internecine strife and factionalism consumed much energy, and activity often was personal rather than goal-oriented. Individual Nationalists, many of them impressive human beings, were right for the wrong reasons. Their aspirations, even emancipation, stemmed from their own ambitions as members of small narrow groups, not from the needs of the vast numbers of Indochinese. They were sympathetic to misery but unable to understand it, hence they did not comprehend the peasant's needs and could not gear their programs to him. They set down the demands of an educated, politicized elite, not those of the poor beset by hunger, isolated by illiteracy, submerged in hopelessness. Communists hold that the key to success in revolution is to correctly identify the enemy; this the Nationalists palpably failed to do.

* The Nationalists lacked vision. They failed to appreciate the value of universal appeals among colonial peoples. Limited in thinking, sometimes possessing little more than a coup d'etat mentality, they tended to treat anticolonialism as a drive to change rulers only, not the need also to create an entirely new set of social institutions.

* The Communists had a more broadly based organizational structure, a superior cadre corps, and a tighter system of internal discipline, chiefly because they always gave priority to organizational and leadership needs. Better trained (with centers outside Indochina providing a steady flow of replacement cadres) and more experienced, the Communists brought to the struggle a kind of skilled revolutionary professionalism that the Nationalists could never match. For this and other reasons having to do with spirit, they developed tough and implacable characteristics that few Nationalists could equal.

* The Communists had a superior strategy, one rooted in the people. It was based on mass action with a premium on organization, identification of the Party with eventual emancipation from French rule, and immediate relief from specific grievances. Every misery was related to foreign rule and coupled to some moderate Party proposal, thus harnessing both psychic and material appeals. The Nationalists had no master plan nor grand strategy. They stood for *doc lap* ("independence") as did most thinking Vietnamese, but this was a largely meaningless abstraction to an illiterate, poverty-ridden villager unless

translated into some important personal concern or material benefit: *doc lap* must mean land availability or tax abatement or low-interest agricultural loans. Initially *doc lap* was the property of the Nationalists. Then it was co-opted by the Communists and subjected to important linguistic manipulation. The Communists made *doc lap*, not a goal, but a way: each small concession wrung from the French was greeted as *doc lap*.

* Marxism-Leninism as an ideological icon, rather than a body of knowledge, was a valuable tool for which the Nationalists had no equivalent. It provided a necessary doctrinal base, but one broad enough to serve both the conservative villager and the intellectual schooled in traditional moral values. The *fact* of communist doctrine was what was important, for it could make anticolonialism legitimate in the eyes of the villager and morally acceptable to the educated. Communist theory, even if incomprehensible to the Vietnamese villager, made the cause respectable—more than mere banditry, as French propagandists maintained.

* The French repressed the Nationalists more severely because they were seen as a clearer enemy. The Nationalists were purely and personally anti-French, while the communist cause was clouded by an abstract hostility to a social system. Also, the Communists had their defenders in the French parliament, which the Nationalists did not.

* Finally there was the natural tendency of all human conditions to polarize and simplify. As a struggle goes on, the extremists grow strong and the center is squeezed out. In Vietnam the struggle—not in the 1930s, but later—came down to a choice between the Communists and the French. The victims in this polarization were the Nationalists.

On balance, the Nationalist-Communist struggle at the end of the decade—for all the gains scored by the Communists—was something of a standoff. No final resolution had been reached. The Nationalists were to lose, but at this point they still could have won. Their defeat was a product of the next page in Vietnamese history, World War II. Here the Communists enjoyed the condition for which they had waited so long: anarchy, in which they could outmaneuver and then destroy the Nationalists.

Chapter 3

World War II: Opportunity

The World War II years—1939–45—were momentous and decisive ones for the Vietnamese communist movement and largely fixed its course for the next generation. A determinist historian would insist that *all* that followed in Vietnam, including final, total communist victory in 1975, flowed from those six years of world war. The war killed colonialism in Asia forever, a fact recognized by all but the French. It destroyed, as all wars do to some degree, the old social order. It created, in Vietnam, the internal disarray, political chaos, social dislocation, and economic crisis that only the Communists were prepared to exploit. The anarchy that came at war's end provided a once-in-history opportunity, the prospect that, with one move in a single moment, the ICP could seize control of all Vietnam.

To understand the Party during the war, it is necessary to consider briefly the major events of World War II as they related to Indochina. The Indochinese peninsula was drawn into the war because of its strategic position. Japan had invaded China nearly a decade before and by 1939 held the entire south China coast. This cut off much Chinese access to foreign sources of war matériel and supplies. The only means of reaching Yunnan, for example, was by way of a railroad that ran from China through Vietnam and back into China and was serviced by Tonkin's major port, Haiphong. The Japanese needed Indochina.

When World War II began in September 1939 (before Japanese entry), the French sought to extract support and aid from her colonies in

Indochina. Thousands of workers and conscripts, as well as some 1.5 million tons of foodstuffs and raw materials, were sent to France. When France collapsed in 1940, Admiral Decoux in Indochina established a local branch of the Vichy government and prepared to sit out the war, determined to preserve the fact and forms of colonialism. To this end he signed, two days after Pearl Harbor, a treaty of cooperation with Imperial Japan.

The Japanese got what they wanted out of Indochina: raw materials, particularly rubber; food (some 3.5 million tons of rice in four years); air and naval bases from which to harrass Allied shipping lanes; and a greater stranglehold on China. The Vichy French, in exchange, got diplomatic recognition of sorts and an extension of life for the colonial system.

Allied interest in Indochina, especially China's portion, centered on the desire to reduce the support being provided Japan and generally to put local military pressure on the Japanese. Efforts were made by the Chinese, Americans, and British to establish local operational units in Indochina that would harrass the Japanese, supply the Allies with intelligence, and aid downed Allied fliers. Some such activity was generated, but it never reached a level that could be called militarily significant. The Japanese confined their occupation of Indochina to the cities and to the crossroads of communication. Japanese presence was thin or nonexistent in the Indochinese countryside, averaging less than one occupation soldier per hamlet. The control mechanism remained in the hands of the French colonial administration. The *colon* saw this as a condition of parity with Japan; the Vietnamese, as a poorly concealed effort to hide French humiliation. Late in the war when Japan assumed direct control of Indochina—the so-called Japanese coup d'etat—replacing, then interning, the French, the final destructive blow to the French position was delivered. So the war was to have tremendous psychological effect on the Vietnamese. It would disgrace the French and discredit their system; this in turn would have great significance for the Party, for it would effectively close the door on Party-French collaboration, that is, on an egalitarian relationship with France, an idea that Ho Chi Minh was to entertain but that the wartime ruin of French status would make impossible.

Finally, World War II was a watershed for the United States in Indochina. The Japanese moved into Indochina, and that brought the

U.S. oil embargo and consequent Japanese humiliation, which in turn opened the road to Pearl Harbor. The postwar heritage left by this chain of events was an American perception of the strategic importance of Indochina, a perception that was to have a considerable role in later fateful decision making.

THE PARTY IN WARTIME

The end of the 1930s found the Party done with the worst decade it would ever experience. Damage inflicted by the Surete had been largely repaired. The humiliating collaboration with the French *colon* imposed by the Comintern became a thing of the past after Hitler attacked the USSR.

The Party's Sixth Plenum met in November 1939 and began a new approach. Leadership was in the hands of Nguyen Van Cu, as secretary general, Le Duan, and Phan Dang Luu. Directives were written fixing the Party's single task as the emancipation of Vietnam from colonialism, the single enemy as imperialism. Officially there was no interest in World War II, since at this moment the Nazi-Soviet pact was still in effect. The Party was to rid Vietnam of all imperialists, French and Japanese alike, and was to do this through the mechanism of a broadened united front. Such Marxist notions as land expropriation were to be downplayed. The Party created the new Indochinese Anti-imperialist People's United Front (Mat Tran Dan Toc Thong Nhat Phan De Dong Duong).

The main significance of the Sixth Plenum was not that it ended the stop-Hitler collaboration—this soon would be reversed—but that it began to shift the strategic center of the struggle against colonialism from the urban proletariat to the rural peasant. To some degree this may have been inadvertent; to some degree it was the result of Maoist influence or example. The organizational overhaul by the plenum resulted in a sophisticated organizational structure—with more persuasive united-front usage and better covert operations—that would prove durable, disciplined, and effective in the environment of the next few years, when something of an organizational vacuum developed in Indochina.

The Party now listed these advantages: it had a dual legal-covert organization; it had a scattered but well-connected network of cells in all major institutions and geographic areas of the country; it had money and some weapons; it had a good intelligence network; and it had a more pragmatic doctrine, having purged itself of the notion of automatic, inevitable victory. There were some losses: the French crackdown ordered as the war began resulted in the arrest and execution of the new secretary general, Nguyen Van Cu, and of long-time Party faithful Le Hong Phong.

The work and doctrinal thought of the Sixth Plenum were advanced at the Seventh Plenum, held in November 1940 with Truong Chinh as acting secretary general and with Hoang Van Thu, Hoang Quoc Viet, Phan Van Luu, and Tran Danh Hinh in attendance. The session was largely devoted to a discussion of the concept of armed struggle, aiming at creating an armed forces nucleus and establishing revolutionary bases, or what were to be called liberation zones.

Organizational challenge to the Party continued throughout the war years. The major opposition, strongest in the South, came from two clusters of Japanese-sponsored collaborationist groups. The first of these was the Dai Viet movement, chiefly the Dai Viet Quoc Dan Dang (Greater Vietnam Nationalist Party), strong in the North and numbering some 25,000 member early in the war; the Dai Viet Dan Chinh (Greater Vietnamese Popular Party), headed by Nguyen Tuong Tam; the Thanh Nien Ai Quoc (Youthful Patriots), led by Vo Xuan Cam; and Phung Xa Quang Gioi (Servants of the Country), headed by Pham Dinh Cuong. The membership of this cluster included many former VNQDD right-wing elements as well as monarchist-oriented Nationalists. The second cluster was composed of Vietnamese who had had prewar contact with Japan (as had many Dai Viet members, of course). It went under several variants of the Phuc Quoc (Restoration) name, most prominent of which was the Viet Nam Phuc Quoc Dong Minh Hoi (Vietnam Restoration League).

Opposition to the Party also came from French collaborationist groups; from the two sociopolitical sects, the Cao Dai and the Hoa Hao; and from the Trotskyist movement, which rejuvenated itself to a degree and reemerged in late 1944 as the October Group (its old internal rival, the Struggle Group, also appeared again, in May 1945), still hostile, of course, to the Stalinist ICP. Finally, as we shall see below, opposition to the Party came from the Nationalist elements supported, if not sponsored, by the KMT.

Apparently the ICP had little traffic with the Chinese Communist Party during World War II; at least available evidence so indicates. Such assistance as the ICP did receive from China came from the KMT. Neither did the ICP get much help from Moscow, mainly because the USSR was preoccupied with survival and also perhaps because the Comintern as an institution had seriously declined.

THE BIRTH OF THE VIET MINH

The Chinese Nationalist government, in its search for ways to intensify pressure on the Japanese, sponsored a meeting at Tsinghai in May 1941 (in advance of which the ICP had staged its Eighth Plenum) for the purpose of creating an effective anti-Japanese campaign in Indochina. The initiative in this undertaking came from a semiautonomous Chinese governor and warlord, Marshal Ching Fa-kwei, and it is therefore not clear how much that eventuated was intended by the KMT central leadership.

Out of the meeting came the Viet Nam Doc Lap Dong Minh Hoi (Vietnamese Independence League), universally termed the Viet Minh. In design it was a united front in the technical sense, an organization of organizations, and included:

* The Indochinese Communist Party

* The ICP's mass or popular organizations, collectively known as the Cuu Quoc (National Salvation) and specifically consisting of the Workers' Cuu Quoc, the Peasants' Cuu Quoc, the Youth's, the Women's, the Elderly People's, the Military Personnel's Cuu Quoc, the Buddhist Monks and Nuns' Cuu Quoc, and the Cultural Cuu Quoc (writers, artists, and intellectuals)

* Elements of the De Cuong Van Hoa Viet Nam (Vietnam Cultural Platform)

* Certain elements of the VNQDD, mostly on an individual basis

* Various other Vietnamese émigrés heading up "ghost" organizations

The Viet Minh adopted a broad anti-French, antiimperialist, antifascist national independence platform. In subsequent official accounts, the historians in Hanoi left no doubt that the Viet Minh was a Party creation:

> The eighth session of the Party Central Committee convened in Pac Bo, Cao Bang province, May 10–19 (1941) under the chairmanship of Comrade Ho Chi Minh . . . and decided to set up a broad united front, the Viet Minh Front, . . . to lead the people to carry out partial uprisings, eventually a general insurrection to win back power throughout the country. Comrade Truong Chinh was elected secretary general of the Party.[1]

The Chinese were not pleased with the results of the meeting and so sponsored a second conference at Luchow in October 1942 at which was created a second front movement, the Viet Nam Cach Mang Dong Minh Hoi (Vietnam Revolutionary League), usually referred to as the Dong Minh Hoi. It was led, nominally at least, by one Nguyen Hai Than, a Vietnamese who had lived in China and served as a general in the KMT army. Membership of the Dong Minh Hoi included elements of the fragmented VNQDD, the Phuc Quoc Dong Minh Hoi, the Dai Viet Quoc Dan Dang, and the Giai Phong Hoi (Liberation League). It also included the Viet Minh, but officially minus the Indochinese Communist Party. Even though the ICP was excluded, leading Party members attended the conference wearing their Viet Minh hats. (Marshal Ching, apparently on central KMT orders, had jailed Ho Chi Minh as a means of keeping him away from the meeting.) The newly formed Dong Minh Hoi was exhorted to get on with its war against the Japanese and was advanced 100,000 Chinese dollars a month to fund its work. But the new group also proved a disappointment, at least to Marshal Ching. The result was a third conference in March 1944. At this point it appears that Marshal Ching, having assessed Ho Chi Minh as the only Vietnamese who could make something of the movement, took matters into his own hands. Ho—then traveling under the name Nguyen Ai Quoc, a name widely and negatively known to the KMT—was advised to change his name, which he did. Marshal Ching then notified the central government that he had found a talented Vietnamese named Ho Chi Minh and suggested that he could lead the Viet Minh. A name check of KMT dossiers revealed, of course, no derogatory information on anyone named Ho Chi Minh, and central approval was granted.

Ho took control of the apparatus at the third conference and did what Marshal Ching thought he could do—breathe life into a moribund organization. Ho created a provisional government that was then imposed on the organizational structure formed in the earlier meetings.

Thus, what finally was created in three conferences was the ICP as a member of a front organization (the Viet Minh), which was part of a broader front (the Dong Minh Hoi) that had been incorporated into a provisional government. How much of this was clear at the time to anyone but Ho Chi Minh is now difficult to determine. Certainly it did not meet the original KMT objectives or expectations. What it did was to hand Ho Chi Minh and the ICP a ready-made organization, enjoying Allied endorsement, for use in pursuing Party interests. Within this Viet Minh/Dong Minh Hoi/Provisional Government edifice was only one institution with fixed plan and purpose, and that was the Indochinese Communist Party.

This plan and purpose had been developed just prior to the first Viet Minh organizational conference, at the Party's Eighth Plenum (May 1941). The plenum was chaired by Ho Chi Minh, back on Vietnamese soil for the first time in thirty years; Truong Chinh was acting secretary general. The theme of the plenum was to prepare for the *thoi co*, "the moment of great opportunity." Out of it came a bold scheme, the grand strategy the Party would follow in virtually a straight line for the next generation.

* The Party was to weather the war as best it could, contributing to the defeat of the Japanese if the cost involved was not too high, but without strengthening the French.

* The Party was to build its force, administratively and organizationally, in preparation for the war's end, when the opportunity to seize power would present itself.

* Party doctrine was to be overhauled and refined into a strategic concept of armed-political struggle, obviously based on the Chinese model but adapted to fit Vietnamese circumstances.

* Preparation for armed struggle involved planning both for insurrection and for general uprising (*khoi nghia*). Armed struggle would be politicized. The chief instrument would be, not the soldier or the

guerrilla, but the armed agitprop team. The leading slogan would be: Politics Is More Important than Military Force. A Command Committee, fledgling military high command, was established under the Central Committee and was composed of Phung Chi Kien, Luong Van Chi (Huy), and Chu Van Tan.

* Political struggle was to be systematized and intensified. This time it would be within a deep united front, the Viet Minh, which became the integral overt element of the Party. Truong Chinh became secretary general of the Viet Minh; ICP members were on its Central Committee. For a time—during all of 1943 and the first half of 1944—Ho Chi Minh personally administered Viet Minh affairs aided by his two chief deputies, Vo Nguyen Giap and Pham Van Dong. The political struggle also spawned two important publications: the *Co giai phong* (Liberation), the Party organ, and *Cuu quoc* (Salvation), the official Viet Minh publication.

A 1943 Party plenum directive stated Party objectives for the middle years of the war:

> (1) Election of a constituent assembly to work out the constitution for a free Indo-China on the basis of adult suffrage; (2) Restoration of democratic liberties and rights, including freedom of organization, press and assembly, freedom of belief and opinion, the right to property, the right of workers to strike, freedom of domicile, and freedom of propaganda; (3) Organization of a national army; (4) Right of minorities to self-determination; (5) Equal rights for women; (6) Nationalization of banks belonging to fascists and the formation of an Indo-Chinese national bank; (7) A strong national economy through development of native industry, communications, agriculture, and commerce; (8) Agricultural reform; (9) Labor legislation, including an eight-hour work day, progressive reform, and social legislation; (10) Development of national education and culture.
>
> In the international sphere the program stands for revision of unequal treaties and an alliance with all democratic nations for the maintenance of peace. More important for the anti-Japanese war, however, is the immediate program of action which is: (1) Organization of the masses—workers, peasants, women, and youth—for the anti-fascist struggle . . . (2) Preparation of an insurrection by the organization of the people into self-defense corps. (3) Formation of guerrilla bands and bases "which will assume greater importance as we gradually approach the time of country-wide military action."[2]

WAR WITH JAPAN

The Viet Minh and the Party pursued the war against Japan by means of both political struggle and armed struggle. From bases along the Chinese border and in the Mekong Delta, Viet Minh elements launched raids and fought skirmishes with Japanese troops, using weapons supplied by the American OSS. The British freed Vietnamese, most of them Communists, from internment on Madagascar and parachuted them into Viet Minh zones. The Viet Minh did help American airmen to get out of Indochina. It did supply the Allies with intelligence. But its military contribution was nominal. Viet Minh forces had only one engagement that could be called strategically important, the battle of Chan Pass (May 1945), in which sixty Japanese were killed.

The Party's main concern was preparation for the future. Japanese control, or even understanding, of the local sociopolitical scene was as superficial as its occupation force was thin. Japanese commanders were content to leave both Nationalists and Communists alone unless they engaged in anti-Japanese activity, which brought swift and brutal retaliation. The Party suffered from the fact that many of its cadres were still in French jails, the Japanese having no interest in releasing them.[3] But Japanese neutrality did provide the Party with what it needed most, time and opportunity to extend and develop its control.

Early in the war the Party was involved in several local insurrections. The first of these—the Bac Son uprising, led by Hoang Van Thu—came when the Japanese entered Vietnam in September 1940. The rout of the French garrison at Bac Son so encouraged local ICP leaders that they staged an uprising. It was suppressed, for the Japanese and the Vichy French quickly agreed to cooperate in quelling Vietnamese resistance. The insurrectionists took to the hills and became the first communist guerrilla units of the war.

Even more significant insurrections were launched in the South. In November 1940 Tran Van Giau and the ICP in Cochin China started an uprising in the My Tho region. It quickly spread to parts of eight Cochin Chinese provinces and culminated in the proclamation of the Indo-chinese Democratic Republic. The uprising lasted about two weeks, then was brutally crushed, with several hundred persons killed and 15,000 imprisoned.

Ho Chi Minh and most other ICP leaders were in Kunming at the time. They tried to stop that uprising and other insurrections as well, predicting that they would fail and that, when they did, the repression to follow would virtually wipe out the ICP. Both predictions proved correct. The 1940 Plain of Reeds rebellion, as it is termed, is treated with particular poignancy by Party historians. Yet they also record that when the Party's Eighth Plenum (May 1941) reviewed the debacle, members realized in their hearts what they had known in their heads, that the greatest danger to the Party was premature violence. The plenum also concluded that only if the Party formed the broadest kind of alliance could it hope to succeed and that it must sacrifice ideological stand for unity. Much Central Committee work during the war years was devoted to discouraging military ventures rather than to launching them. The committee made every effort to preserve Party assets at the basic level; when it was necessary to squander casualties in some armed struggle gesture, non-Party people were used. As late as November 1944 the Party reprimanded cadres in the Nhai-Dinh Ca region for their military adventurism, insisting that the time still had not come for an insurrection.

In spite of this caution, building a military force did proceed apace during the war years. Initially, this consisted of decentralized guerrilla bands. The original military organization, forerunner of what would become the People's Army of Vietnam (PAVN), was the First National Salvation Platoon, formed in Bac Son in September 1940. Its commanding officer was Phung Chi Kien. The Second Platoon was formed in Bac Son in September 1941 and the Third Platoon in Tuyen Quang in February 1944. The first formal military units did not appear until December 1944 with the establishment of the Vietnam Liberation Army Agitprop Unit (Doi Viet Nam Tuyen Truyen Giai Phong Quan), the so-called armed propaganda teams. These were well named. They were armed, but for purposes of defense and intimidation, and not to seek out combat. Their primary task was to enter Vietnamese villages and do organizational and motivational work. They were to prepare for the future, not fight the war:

> Uncle Ho issued a decree on December 22, 1944, organizing the Armed Agit-Prop force under the leadership of Vo Nguyen Giap. These troops followed the principle: Politics are more important than military forces. These troops fanned out from the highlands to the lowlands to open the phase of combined armed struggle and political struggle.[4]

By the end of 1944 the Viet Minh had several thousand armed troops, under the name of the National Salvation Army.

THE AUGUST REVOLUTION

The war against Japan ended unexpectedly—only a few persons knew of the atomic bomb and the probability that it would bring a quick termination to the war—catching all participants in the Indochina drama by surprise.

Suddenly Vietnam was a military vacuum and in total anarchy; it had no government. Japanese troops, numbed by defeat, stood immobilized awaiting repatriation, caring nothing about Vietnam or its future. French officials and troops were in internment camps where they had been placed by the Japanese four months earlier. There was a Vietnamese government, established by the Japanese and headed by Bao Dai, but it was little more than a few individuals living in Hue.[5] No Allied troops were in the country. Hastily, plans were made to divide the country at the sixteenth parallel and, for purposes of disarming the Japanese, to assign the southern half to the British (from India) and the northern half to the Chinese. In any event, it would be weeks before Allied troops in any strength could be gotten into place throughout Indochina.

For the Vietnamese Communists, the decisive hour had arrived. In anticipation of Japanese defeat—although it came sooner than expected—Ho Chi Minh and his top Party associates had spent the summer planning their course of action. The Central Committee had met on March 9, 1945, at Dinh Bang outside of Hanoi and issued (March 12) a series of directives, the most famous entitled "French-Japanese confrontation and our policies" (Nhat Phap Ban Nhau va hanh dong cua chung ta). In the name of the Viet Minh, these directives ordered:

* Preparation of a fixed geographic base area, to be called a liberation zone. This was formally created in early June and consisted of six Tonkin provinces: Cao Bang, Bac Can, Lang Son, Thai Nguyen, Tuyen Quang, and Ha Giang.

* Establishment of a series of liberation committees (or popular committees) to assume local temporary administrative control. In concept, they were akin to the Paris Commune or the later Shanghai Commune.

* Integration of the various guerrilla bands, armed propaganda teams, and other armed struggle elements into a single military command. This order was formalized at the Bac Ky Revolutionary Military Conference in April, chaired by Truong Chinh, which created the Vietnam Liberation Army (Viet Nam Giai Phong Quan) under the command of Vo Nguyen Giap and his two chief aides, Chu Van Tan and Van Tien Dung. A crash training program for village-level revolutionaries was launched immediately.

* Preparation of plans to seize Japanese military stocks and food stores. (The country was entering a time of serious famine. Party history later claimed that two million people starved to death in 1945.)[6]

* Detailed planning for mass political action in the cities and for general mobilization of the population.

On August 9, the day after Hiroshima, the Central Committee met at Tan Trao and ordered, for the following week beginning August 13, what came to be called the August Revolution. This meeting also elected a Central National Liberation Committee (Uy Ban Dan Toc Giai Phong Trung Uong), which within two weeks was to become a provisional government; a week after that, the new government of Vietnam.

The Viet Minh met in congress on the sixteenth and issued a basic position paper embodying the famed Ten-Point Program (mentioned earlier as the Party objectives set forth after the plenum in 1943).

Thus, the stage was set for seizure of power. However many loose ends remained, the Party obviously was ahead of all other contenders. Viet Minh forces entered prostrate Hanoi on August 19 and took control, firing only a few symbolic revolver shots in the process. Tran Huy Lieu went to Hue and persuaded Bao Dai to abdicate on August 23 and to join the Viet Minh as a private citizen. A united-front group took control of Saigon on August 25. On September 2, in Ba Dinh park in Hanoi, Ho Chi Minh read the Vietnamese Declaration of Independence and proclaimed the birth of the Democratic Republic of Vietnam.[7]

This was the August Revolution. Actually, it was not a revolution as that term is normally applied.[8] A government (Japanese) was on the way out, another (Allied) was on its way in temporarily, and a third (French) was expected to return. In the interim, Ho and the Party moved into the political vacuum with something between a coup d'etat and the simple act of picking up unopposed the reins of power. The purpose of this strategy, and the reason for the haste, was to present the Allies, who did not arrive for three weeks, with a de facto political situation. Ho probably knew he could not prevent return of the French no matter what kind of government he established, but he calculated that the stronger an interim governing arrangement he could make, the better would be his later bargaining position. But the myth of the August Revolution was born and now is firmly entrenched in Vietnamese minds: the people overthrew the ruling government; they set up and made fully operational a new government, only later to have it physically taken from them by a French invasion aided by the British and Chinese.

The French did return—proclaiming officially, "We have come to reclaim our heritage"—and began at once to reinstate the kind of government that ruled in prewar days. The British, in the South, kept order as best they could, plagued by complex street battles staged by French, Trotskyists, Stalinists, and the Cao Dai and Hoa Hao. The British departed as soon as they could do so with dignity. In the North, as most Vietnamese had anticipated, the arriving Chinese were not content simply to supervise the repatriation of the Japanese and then leave. The KMT, fully recognizing its coming death struggle with the Chinese Communists, sought to create in northern Vietnam a condition of support and strength, working through the Dong Minh Hoi (led by Nguyen Hai Than), other VNQDD elements and, in fact, any anti-Communist Vietnamese willing to collaborate. Its efforts were backed by 50,000 troops in Hanoi.

Extensive writings by Party historians later listed their reasons for success in the August Revolution: (a) careful advance preparation, good organization of Party and military, a sound ideological foundation already fixed, a resistance base to fall back on that gave a sense of confidence to participants; (b) proper timing—the Party waited for the opportune moment; (c) use of the right instrument, the national united front which incorporated virtually all political activists and supporters and harnessed the people's energies and raised their revolutionary consciousness; (d) use of the armed-political struggle concept, which was destined to become a new way of making war; and (e) pioneer use of new psychological warfare techniques, such as the *binh van* ("action among the military"), the proselyting campaign.

For the Party, much had been accomplished, but much remained. Immediate tasks were obvious: to get rid of the occupiers, to nullify the strength of indigenous opposition, and then, by some combination of armed and political struggle, to force out the French. Clearly this meant, sooner or later, full-scale war.

Chapter 4

Leadership

In terms of personnel, the history of the Vietnamese communist movement is very largely the history of two figures: the individual known to the world as Ho Chi Minh,[1] and that anonymous composite, the Party cadre. Without Ho, the course of Vietnamese history would have been vastly different. Without the Party cadre, Vietnamese communism would have had little history at all.

HO CHI MINH

The life of Ho Chi Minh, so intimately bound up in the history of the Party, is discussed passim throughout this work. Suffice it here to set down the major highlights of his career.[2]

He went abroad in 1911 as a messboy aboard the S.S. *Admiral Latouche Treveille*. His departure from Vietnam, it appears, was not primarily a political act—to search for Vietnam's destiny, as official history would have us believe—but a result of the more or less normal wanderlust of the bolder and more imaginative young. For years he wandered without much purpose, pursuing various occupations to sustain himself—photo retoucher, writer, kitchen hand, seaman, translator, janitor—until he found the calling for which he was uniquely suited: organization man in left-wing, and later communist, circles.

Ho became radicalized during World War I, as did millions of Europeans. Lenin had just worked a political miracle in Russia. Ho witnessed a general strike in Milan and the work of Paris radicals, London anarchists, and Irish revolutionaries. It was a time of turmoil, and many, in and out of radical circles, believed world revolution was at hand. Ho joined the French Socialist Party, traveled through France as an agitator, pamphleteered at the Versailles Conference. When the French Socialist Party split at its November 1920 Tours meeting over the issue of affiliation with the Communist Third International, Indochinese delegate Ho opted for the left wing, which broke and established the French Communist Party under Marcel Cachin. Ho became a charter member and spent the next five years working between Paris and Moscow. He organized the Intercolonial Union and the Vietnamese Patriots Group[3] and edited three periodicals, the *Pariah*, *Soul of Vietnam*, and *Nguoi cung kho* (Proletariat). In Moscow he was elected a member of the Central Committee of the Krestintern (Peasant International), a front organization of agrarian groups willing to collaborate with the Comintern. He attended the Fifth Communist International (June 1924) as a delegate. He published a study of French colonialism.[4] Apparently he left the USSR for China in 1938, the time of the purge trials.

As noted earlier, Ho, as a full Comintern agent, went with the Borodin mission to Canton in 1925 under general instructions to do Party recruiting and organizational work in Southeast Asia—Thailand (Siam) and Singapore, as well as Indochina. He created the Thanh Nien, then in 1930 the Indochinese Communist Party. He was detained by the British in Hong Kong in 1931 and deported a year later under somewhat peculiar circumstances.[5]

The 1930s are nearly blank. Official biographers offer nothing; others dispute. Apparently, part of the time was spent in Moscow: at the Seventh Comintern Congress (1935), at the Institute for National and Colonial Questions, then at the postgraduate Lenin School in 1936. Some writers report that he was jailed by Stalin for several years during the period—this was the time of the purge trials—while others believe he spent the remainder of the decade in China.

Ho appeared in May 1941 at the organizational meeting of the Viet Minh, but his early association with this group was interrupted by a period in a KMT prison. The remainder of World War II was spent in China, Ho returning to Vietnam in time for the August Revolution in 1945.

During the Viet Minh War years, Ho guided the cause of war, Party, and government from his mountain headquarters north of Hanoi. After the July 1954 Geneva Conference, which ended the war and divided Vietnam, Ho, in the following year, was elected president of the Democratic Republic of Vietnam (DRV). Subsequently he held, for varying periods, other major governmental and Party posts: prime minister, chairman of the National Defense Council, Party secretary, and chairman of the Party Central Committee. He died of a cerebral hemorrhage on September 3, 1969, at the age of seventy-nine.

Ho was, from the earliest days, a prominent (if not important) figure in the world communist movement. In Europe he had a singular, even exotic image. Later, he was still more attractive to the European left, as Ho the giant killer, the avenging force from out of Asia. He knew most of the early Marxists and other radicals: Trotsky, Bukharin, Zinoviev, Radek, Dimitrov, Borodin, Vassily Bluecher, Chou En-lai (at Whampoa), M. N. Roy, Sen Katayama, Marcel Cachin, Marius Moutet, and Léon Blum—but not, apparently, Lenin. Nor did he meet Stalin until after he became DRV chief of state. This indicates Ho's place in the early communist hierarchy as that of an important, even high-level, member of the Asian communist movement, but it was a qualified place in that Asia itself ranked low in the Comintern scheme of things. Vietnam scarcely received any consideration at all. For years it was a mere appendage of the French Communist Party. To the extent that Asia did figure in Comintern thinking—and little material on the subject appears in official publications of the 1920s and 1930s—it was China, not Vietnam.[6] Ho might have been a mover and shaker in Asia, but he was a lone, odd voice in Moscow. He was useful to the Comintern as an agent, but his missions, by their nature, were marginal in terms of the Comintern's global view. Ho entered world communism's pantheon much later than official DRV history would have it. Only after he had won power through a victory in the Viet Minh War did his fellow communist leaders around the world take full note of him.

Ho's association with Marxism, as opposed to Marxists, is harder to fix. Official biographies maintain that he was an orthodox communist from the earliest days.

> Uncle Ho went abroad in 1911 and . . . progressed from patriotism to communism. . . . Someone said that President Ho was a born revolutionary, an innate Marxist. We understand this as praise of his crystal-clear revolutionary quality and unusually profound political views.

Since his first contact with Marxism-Leninism and the proletarian revolution, Uncle Ho was an indefatigable and knowledgeable proponent of Marxism-Leninism.

[Ho] was the first Vietnamese to creatively apply Marxism-Leninism to the conditions of our country. . . . [Ho] was not only a great patriot but an outstanding fighter in the international Communist movement. . . .[7]

Ho himself wrote:

In the beginning it was patriotism and not communism that induced me to believe in Lenin and the Third International. But little by little, progressing step by step in the course of the struggle and combining theoretical studies of Marxism-Leninism with practical activities, I came to realize that socialism and communism alone are capable of emancipating workers and downtrodden people all over the world.[8]

At the end, in his final testament, Ho wrote that he "goes now to join Marx, Lenin, and the other revolutionary elders."[9]

Marxism-Leninism, as a body of knowledge, could hardly have had much influence on him in his formative and impressionable early years. As far as is known, he had no association with it in school, and even later, when he was abroad, there was no authoritative communist analysis of the Vietnamese colonial scene. Neither Marx nor Lenin wrote about Vietnam. The text most applicable was the Second Comintern's "Thesis on the National and Colonial Question" (1920), but by its advent Ho probably had moved beyond it in his own thinking, with his conviction that the revolution must be two-stage—first nationalist-bourgeois, then proletarian-party—that the Party could cooperate with nationalist-bourgeois elements in temporary alliance providing the Party strictly maintained its own sense of identity and retained a monopoly association with the proletariat. Ahead of Mao by several years, Ho argued that the best means of destroying capitalist societies was by a series of debilitating colonial wars of liberation, not through urban labor agitation. This he set forth at the Fifth Comintern Congress in 1924. It drew no response and little interest and, in any event, was contrary to accepted Marxist dogma.

It can be argued—and is argued by some—that Ho initially was not a doctrinaire communist but a communist-nationalist amalgam. To a degree this is a matter of semantics. Ho was loyal to the communist system and obeyed Comintern orders unhesitatingly, yet he managed to have orders issued him that were in Vietnam's (and his) interests. Dogma did not inhibit his action, nor did he ever sacrifice much for the Comintern. He did not see the issue as a choice between nationalism or communism, and his being a nationalist therefore did not contradict the fact that he also was a communist. Ho saw communism as an extraordinarily effective means of furthering nationalist interests. It had sound strategy, brilliant organizational techniques, and it answered all important questions. Hence, he embraced it as a national communist. In his day that was perhaps unique, but today the world is full of national communists.

Ho's connection with communism, then, was not doctrinal so much as it was pragmatic loyalty. His model was not the abstract vision of Marx and Lenin but the very real communist model of the KMT (largely the brainchild of Mikhail Borodin). It was here, with the Borodin example in Canton, that Ho came to grips with the fact of communism. His conclusion was that only the Borodin adaptation of the Leninist formula for revolution—and all that the combination represented—could guarantee success. It required total, undeviating loyalty, which he gave. But it was not loyalty to an ideology, for Ho was no true believer. Nor was it loyalty based on the psychological satisfaction of commitment, for Ho was too self-contained for that. Rather, it was loyalty stemming from realization that only allegiance to a system would deliver victory. Once this idea was fixed, Ho's life, and indeed the history of Vietnam, assumed a logic of its own. His cause was anticolonialism. When colonialism was defeated and the French expelled, the cause was transformed from self-determination to monopoly of power for the Party. The name of the cause was not changed; anticolonialism was simply redefined. The struggle went on, now against Vietnamese, a struggle for power for its own sake, the fate of all goal-oriented political movements once they become successful. Noble anticolonialism turned into one more episode in the history of power-hungry despotism. Quite possibly Ho did not want it to turn out that way.

Truong Chinh's biography of Ho, probably the most authoritative official study that will be written in our era, assigns Ho the role in history of initial impetus. He was, Truong Chinh writes, the first Vietnamese to discover the correct revolutionary line for Vietnam and to build around it an effective organization. Using Marxism-Leninism as a compass, Ho correctly analyzed Vietnamese society, established the class-based nature of the revolution, fixed its main driving forces, and eliminated the adventurism and individualistic heroism that weakened earlier revolutionary movements. Once the cause was launched—by which is meant 1930 or, at the latest, 1945—the various immutable forces of history took over, and these, not Ho, became the operative determinants. After that Ho was a sort of national character reference whose contribution was to set a personal example for the faithful. Truong Chinh writes that he then "lived for everyone else. He worried about the worry of others. He rejoiced in the joy of others. He also worried before others and always wanted everyone else to be joyful before he was joyful. . . . He set the example of industriousness, thrift, integrity, and righteousness, the person who did everything for the public and kept nothing for himself."[10]

This treatment, now common from Hanoi historians, reduces Ho to an unbelievable model of virtue, a portrait so simplistic that it borders on caricature. Whatever his inner nature, it is clear that Ho Chi Minh's personality was not the simple, one-dimensional, avuncular saint cast by his official biographers.

What then is to be struck on the balance sheet for Ho Chi Minh? As with most world figures, his success largely defies rational explanation, filled as it is with the implausible. We can note several major characteristics of his personality: he was a wanderer, a searcher, and, as such, a survivor; he was a westernized colonial; he was a bold gambler; he was uniquely (but not ideologically) educated; above all, he was a skilled organization man. Much credit for his success goes to his being Vietnamese, to the peculiar qualities of his people that he put to good use. He blended these with the temper of the Vietnamese times, being acutely sensitive to the national consciousness of his countrymen. He recognized the centrality of image in modern life and at all times projected the correct one—benevolent uncle come to put things right. He maintained a clean background (or at least an unknown one) when virtually all other Vietnamese leaders were becoming tarnished. Much of his success must be credited to his personal qualities, his self-discipline, his asceticism, his selfless dedication, and his immunity (or indifference) to the lures of nepotism, high living, and corruption. Finally, he had a large share of gambler's success, what the world calls luck.

It seems reasonably clear that history will judge the success of the Vietnamese communist movement as a product of superior organization and correct leadership, and that there probably would not have been that success without the unique contributions of Ho Chi Minh.

OTHER LEADERS

Ho Chi Minh was the central element in the leadership structure. Around him were four major figures who made up the inner circle: Truong Chinh, Le Duan, Vo Nguyen Giap, and Pham Van Dong. Briefly, they can be described as follows:

Truong Chinh (b. 1907, Nam Dinh province, as Dang Xuan Khu), the Party theoretician generally credited with devising the armed-political struggle strategy that defeated the French. Less educated than other early major Party figures (he attended a post–high school French program in commerce for one or two years), he learned his Marxism-Leninism from smuggled materials while in Con Son prison; so adept was he that he soon became the prison's chief indoctrinator. After the Viet Minh War he masterminded the disastrous social reconstruction period and, to a degree, fell from power. He made a comeback in the early 1960s. For years he served as chairman of the National Assembly Standing Committee, making the assembly and the Fatherland Front (with which it is associated), plus the country's intellectuals, his power base. Commonly described, but without substantiation, as pro-Chinese, Truong Chinh has a reputation for ultramilitancy, even fanaticism, also probably undeserved. He does seem to take ideas more seriously, however, than do most of his fellow Politburo members. Certainly his writings—*August Revolution, The Resistance Will Win,* and especially *Primer for Revolt* (the best book ever written by a Vietnamese Communist)—are more innovative, contributive, and full of ideas than the writings of all the rest of the Politburo combined.

Le Duan (b. 1908, Quang Tri province), the railroad clerk who rose to rule the Vietnamese communist movement after the death of Ho Chi Minh. His power came not because of his brilliance or his political skills but because he is a careful administrator, a nimble-footed policy implementer, and, given his abilities as a manipulator, something of a substitute Ho Chi Minh. His constituency originally was southern Party cadres, now is most of the Party cadre corps. His career has been marked by a series of misfortunes that have somehow failed to destroy him. The French imprisoned him for subversion in 1931, sentencing him to twenty years. He was released in 1936 and in that year joined the ICP. Rearrested in the 1940 sweep-up of Communists, he was sentenced to ten years in prison, released in August 1945. Early in the Viet Minh

War, he became close to Ho Chi Minh as his chief organizer and Party administrator. After reportedly demanding more challenging duty, he went South in 1949 either as military commander or political commissar (depending on one's source) and served for about six years. Then he was ordered back to Hanoi, the explanation for which varies. One report is that he was relieved of his command because of poor generalship (and replaced by Le Duc Tho); the other explanation says he was called home to take over Party management, chosen because he was the only ranking Party leader not tarred by the land-reform scandal. He continued to press for a militant line in the South and thus has been identified as a southerner (actually he is a centerite). He struggled with Truong Chinh over doctrine and for preeminent position under Ho. Le Duan effectively took control of the Party in 1957 and was named first secretary in 1960. After Ho's death he moved away from his theoretician image as well as from his ultra-pro-South position. He became a Party generalist, administrator, fixer, eventually the Party's number one official, at least "first among equals."

Vo Nguyen Giap (b. 1911, Quang Binh province), also known as Tran Van Lam and Anh Van, the Party's principal military figure. The son of an impoverished mandarin of lower rank, Giap reportedly began his radical activities as a Thanh Nien messenger at the Haiphong electric power plant, later becoming a Tan Viet in Hue high school. Educated at Hanoi University (he tutored students privately and received financial aid from his future father-in-law, Dang Thai Mai), he received a degree roughly equivalent to an M.A. but failed his fourth-year examination for a higher degree. He later taught history, became active in Party affairs, and then came into prominence late in World War II when he created the People's Army of Vietnam (PAVN), building it from a thirty-four-man guerrilla unit in 1944 to a million-man force (including militia) that ultimately conquered all of Vietnam in 1975. During this entire period Giap dominated the DRV military scene, as secretary of the Central Military Party Committee, deputy premier for national defense, and commander in chief of the armed forces. Within the military he enjoyed unquestioned loyalty, unchallenged leadership. At the Politburo level he debated doctrine frequently with Truong Chinh. Western military analysts rate him a mediocre strategist but a brilliant logistician, able to move men and matériel around a battlefield far faster than anyone has a right to expect. Bernard Fall called him a genius as logistics general. His victory at Dien Bien Phu, whatever the reasons for it, assures his place as chief military hero in early Party history. Reportedly a lonely man—his wife died in a French prison and his only sister is said to have been executed by the French—he was in poor health during the last years of the Vietnam War and day-to-day military command gradually passed to General Van Tien Dung, his deputy.

Pham Van Dong (b. 1906, Quang Ngai province), the polished, urbane Party figure and single-minded administrator (whose personality has been compared to Chou En-lai's) who created the DRV bureaucracy, under Ho's tutelage, and ran it for more than three decades. The son of a Hue mandarin, his formal education, at Ho's suggestion, was extended by study at the Whampoa Military Academy in China. Then followed six years in prison, after conviction on student agitation charges. Dong was Ho Chi Minh's early and closest associate and the only member of the present-day Politburo who knew Ho in China in the 1920s, the rest meeting him in 1940. They worked well together. Dong, of no strong personality, became the loyal follower ("my faithful companion," as Ho expressed it), yet also the tough-minded implementer of Ho's organizational and administrative dreams. Frequently described as pro-Soviet and superhawk, Dong probably deserves neither of those characterizations. He served as DRV prime minister for decades and as the country's principal early negotiator with external powers. Not being a leader in the full sense, Dong tended to fade after Ho's death, although continuing to serve as chief director of the state's affairs.

Other major figures on the Party scene after the takeover of power included:

* Pham Hung (b. 1912, Vinh Long province), also know as Pham Van Thien; the victorious general in the South in the final years of the Vietnam War. From a gentry family in the South (near My Tho), Hung was a Thanh Nien and then an early member, perhaps a founder, of the ICP. He was sentenced to death in 1931 (later commuted) and spent most of the 1930s and World War II in prison or under house arrest. A Pham Von Dong protégé, Hung was a guerrilla leader, first in the North, then, during the Viet Minh War, in the South. He was the only true southerner (that is, Cochin Chinese) in the Third Congress Politburo.

* Le Duc Tho (b. 1910, Nam Ha province), the Party's first teacher. Originally in competition with Le Duan, superseding him as chief Party official in the South during the Viet Minh War, Tho eventually

was outpaced by his rival. He served as director of the Party's Organization Department, which recruits and trains cadres and develops
and reindoctrinates middle-ranking cadres in specialized Party schools.
He managed the Paris talks during the Vietnam War chiefly because
of his knowledge of southern affairs. He is regarded as an important
swing force in Politburo decision making.

* Hoang Van Hoan (b. 1905, Nghe An province), an old-guard Party
member and the Party's principal advisor on the Sino-Soviet dispute
and on foreign policy in general. A Thanh Nien member and then
founder of the ICP, he had a long and close association with Ho Chi
Minh and later worked closely with Truong Chinh. Hoan served in
China for years, in liaison work during the 1930s and later as DRV
ambassador to the People's Republic of China (PRC). He has a reputation as a Maoist militant and is believed by many to be the most influential official Vietnamese among the Chinese. In recent years he
has been active as vice chairman of the National Assembly Standing
Committee and its attendant Fatherland Front.

* Nguyen Duy Trinh (b. 1910, Nghe An province), the veteran revolutionary turned nation builder. Since 1965, as DRV foreign minister,
he has been identified with external affairs, but Trinh is an economist
by training and is responsible for such national development as went
on in the DRV in the period between the Viet Minh and the Vietnam
wars. Earlier he rescued the land-reform program. He is regarded
as a good planner, both as theoretician and implementer, who developed the economic base (including foreign aid programs) to support
the Viet Minh War. His transfer in 1965 from head of the State Planning Commission to foreign affairs apparently was because of the Politburo's calculation that with little economic development during the
war, Trinh's services were better employed elsewhere.

* Le Thanh Nghi (b. 1911, Hanoi), the economic agitprop cadre turned
foreign aid fund-raiser. He also was trained as an economist but early
moved into motivational work in the economic sector in charge of pro-
moting and administering emulation campaigns to ensure that production norms were met. He served as director of the Party's Emulation
Department, which ran the vast Stakhanovite campaigns. In the mid-
1960s he began devoting most of his time to soliciting economic and
military aid abroad.

* Tran Quoc Hoan (b. 1910, Thai Binh province), the Party's policeman. Hoan served as Hanoi-Haiphong Party secretary during the Viet Minh War, later worked with Le Duan to reestablish Party authority after the troubles of 1956 and to enforce the unpopular agricultural commune system. He is the DRV's first and only minister of public security, having held the post since the inception of the ministry in 1953. His mentor is Pham Von Dong. He is regarded as a technical, rather than political, Party figure and is prized by his fellow Politburo members for his ability to assure internal security in firm but inconspicuous ways.

* Van Tien Dung (b. 1917, Ha Dong province), the DRV's superspy (strategic intelligence chief) who gradually moved into position as overall commander of the DRV's military forces. Dung joined the ICP in the 1930s, served as senior political commissar during the Viet Minh War, and became highly regarded (as he still is) as a political rather than professional general. In thirty years service in the PAVN he has risen in the ranks of the Central Military Party Committee, whose chief concerns are external intelligence, internal counterintelligence, and internal troop morale and indoctrination. He became second in command to General Giap during the Vietnam War and gradually assumed more and more routine control as Giap's health worsened. Dung wrote a remarkably candid book, *Great Spring Victory*, in 1976, describing the last days of the Vietnam War from the communist side.

* Nguyen Chi Thanh (b. 1915, Nghe An province), an important military figure and director of the war in the South until his death in 1967, reportedly in an air raid. Truong Chinh was his mentor, and Thanh's death shifted the Politburo balance somewhat against Truong Chinh.

* Tran Van Giau, French-educated, Moscow-trained southerner, of great dedication and intellectuality, he also was the most bloody-handed of early Party figures and was responsible for the deaths of dozens of Party enemies and Party deviants. He served as Party secretary in the difficult 1931–35 period and later operated in the South. During the Viet Minh War he ran Party affairs in Laos and Cambodia, where his ruthless methods became so repugnant even to hardened top Party figures as to cause him to lose status and then power in the hierarchy. He drifted into obscurity, receiving only minor diplomatic and educational assignments, reportedly dying in Hanoi in 1969 at the age of fifty-nine.

* Nguyen Van Tao, a southerner who went from Saigon to Paris in the 1920s and joined the French Communist Party in 1927. An early associate of Ho Chi Minh, Tao later became a major Party figure in Cochin China and leader of the anti-Trotskyist campaign there. He was a member of the Viet Minh government as minister of labor and was active in southern affairs as a member of the DRV National Assembly's Reunification Committee. He died in 1970.

* Nguyen Van Cu (b. 1912, Ha Bac province), early Party hero, one of its first organizers in the Tonkin region and a pioneer figure in the development of the Party's *kiem thao* ("self-criticism") institution. Cu was expelled from school for revolutionary activities, joined the Thanh Nien, and did organizational work in the Mao Khe coal mines. He was arrested in 1930, released in 1936, became a Central Committee member in 1937 and Party secretary general in 1938, operating out of Saigon. Cu reportedly recruited Le Duan into the Party. He wrote *Kiem thao* in 1939, and it became a Party handbook. Arrested by the French in June 1940, Cu was executed in May 1941.

Four early figures who appear to have lost power are Hoang Quoc Viet, Ha Huy Giap, Ton Duc Thang, and Nguyen Luong Bang, all of whom were Politburo members in the 1950s and then dropped from that level. Finally, early records list Nguyen Duc Canh (executed by the French in 1932), Nguyen Phong Sac, Do Ngoc Du, and Trinh Dinh Cuu, little being known about any of them.

LEADERSHIP CHARACTERISTICS

The Vietnamese Communist Party leadership elite—that is, the Central Committee as well as its inner Politburo—has proven to be the most durable ruling communist group anywhere. Indeed, it is probably the most long-lived group of rulers in modern times. The small band of men, forged together in the crucible years, continuously, with virtually unchanged personnel, ruled communist Vietnam for three decades. The powerful of the Viet Minh years, with minor exceptions, became the anointed in the new Democratic Republic of Vietnam. The thirteen men of the Politburo named at the 1960 Third Party Congress formed a power monolith that operated throughout the entire Vietnam War. No one was added to the elite group and, save for two claimed by death, the structure went unchanged for twenty-five years. No other society in the modern world has been ruled for so long by so few. Stability then, has been the major characteristic of Vietnam's leadership. Another important one was the nonproletarian background of most top leaders. In fact, the majority were not even from the middle class (which hardly existed in colonial Vietnam anyway) but came from mandarin, gentry, or intellectual/professional backgrounds. Pham Van Dong came from a mandarin family. Truong Chinh and Vo Nguyen Giap received more education than did most Vietnamese of the time. Pham Hung's family was gentry, as was Nguyen Luong Bang's. Hoang Van Hoan came from a land-owning family. Ho Chi Minh came from a prominent family distantly related to Vietnamese royalty. What distinguished these early Party leaders from their fellow Vietnamese—in and out of the Party—was education; they were among the few who were educated, surrounded by a vast mass who were not.[11]

The driving forces in their lives became twofold: anticolonialism and the modernization of Vietnam using a socialist/communist model.

Thus in various ways these early top leaders were remarkably similar in background, in education, in outlook. Small wonder a close old-boy network developed. All came to the Party in their youth. Together they went through the traumas of their times and emerged a tightly knit band of veterans. No postrevolutionary figures here.

They regard ideology as icon. No ideological innovators, they are doctrinally conservative. In public statements they appear closer to USSR than to PRC thinking, but it may simply be that they are more orthodox than Maoist. They embrace a consistent, orthodox, and in some ways quaintly antiquated brand of communism, clinging to communist tradition while the rest of the communist world moves on to new considerations. The result of their influence is to impose a deadly sterility on ideology within the Party.

THE CADRE

An outsider investigating Vietnamese communism finds that a compelling mystique surrounds the unique institution known as the Party cadre. In idealized form, at least, the Party cadre is a social superman, the talented, dedicated, selfless individual who works tirelessly to improve society. He is tough and incorruptible, yet human, holding perfection as his only standard. He is the personification of what a modern complex society needs to operate properly, indeed, to survive. We have no equivalent in our non-Marxist society—neither the professional bureaucrat in any of his three forms within the government (civil service, military service, or foreign service) nor the activist/volunteer outside the government is a true counterpart. Perhaps the closest in image is the old-time American trade-union organizer.

The communist cadre is a combination priest, policeman, and editorial writer. He is the link between the center and the individual. He translates Party directives into reality in the village, commune, and factory, then makes them work. He motivates, energizes, communicates, and, above all, organizes. He carries the major burden of the revolution. He is whipping boy for official failure, target for constant criticism from above and endless complaint from below. He is harassed and overworked, sometimes incompetent or corrupt. He is what makes the system work.

Specifically, *cadre* is the generic term for the Party official found between the Central Committee in Hanoi and the basic-level organizations. But cadre is more than an individual; it is a way of ruling a society that is without the franchise. Cadre structure can be thought of as a pyramid sliced horizontally into three sections: the national cadres; the intermediate, or secondary-level, cadres; and the lower-echelon, or tertiary, cadres. The ratio among them is about 1:10:40. The secondary-level cadre is the chief instrument for policy implementation, responsible for translating the leadership's orders into reality. He is oriented toward the center, upward to the Central Committee, while the tertiary-level cadre is oriented downward and chiefly concerned with membership at the basic level. Cadre strength in 1975 was estimated to be 200,000 (4,000–5,000 national-level, 40,000–50,000 intermediate-level, and the rest tertiary-level cadres), although some observers insist the total was lower, around 120,000 cadres. If the higher figure is accepted, and the estimate of total Party strength is about 1.5 million, cadres account for about 14 percent of the total Party strength.

Essentially *cadre* is a functional term related to specific activity; thus there are organizational cadres, agitprop cadres, economic cadres, scientific cadres, and so on. Often it is difficult to distinguish between a cadre and a technician. One does not become a cadre simply by virtue of a functional assignment nor cease being one upon leaving a particular assignment. As one defecting cadre in the South told the author: "You are a cadre because of what you are or what you do or how others regard you."

To a degree, this is a social class if the standard definition is accepted (*social class:* social rank based on social status). As such, it is a new class in Vietnamese society. Within it are three unofficial but very real social ranks that in turn determine status: (a) upper-rank, elite, general-leadership cadres (perhaps 5 percent of the total); (b) middle-rank, scientific and technical cadres who have steadily assumed greater status in recent years (about 40 percent); and (c) the lowest-ranking, administrative (or linking) cadres in the mass organizations (about 40 percent). Each cadre has a Party association (or career), of course, but also a professional career in some institution—such as a military unit, a factory, a hospital—that also helps fix his status. Each of these two careers—Party and profession—impinges on the other. Status is also determined by personal reputation, Party honors, professional accomplishment, and influential personal or familial associations. Older cadres, the so-called Old Comrades, often hold unofficial but extraordinarily high status. These are the veterans who have been through it all and who are respected, venerated, and (they complain) ignored by the younger cadres.

Through the years the Party has developed what might be called the idealized cadre profile:

* He is a master of the techniques of mobilization, that is, skillful in dealing with people in groups. His ability to motivate is a matter more of psychology than of ideology and a product of experience rather than of education.

* He is zealously ideological, class-conscious, egalitarian-minded, proletarian-oriented. He is Red, that is, a Communist who identifies closely with the masses, rather than one who simply has absorbed the Marxist-Leninist body of knowledge, and who has arrived at that state intuitively rather than intellectually.

* He is self-disciplined, ascetic, one who lives a clean, frugal, simple life and who is idealistic to the point of naïveté.

* He is loyal and obedient and does not question the philosophic underpinnings of his society. He will not innovate in obeying orders, although he is expected to use ingenuity in finding ways to carry them

out. He never exceeds his orders, for there is no room in the system for the pioneer venturing beyond limits set by the Party.

* He is substantively or professionally skilled, that is, expert as well as Red. He is technically proficient in something. He is expected to undergo extensive and continual training and retraining in doctrinal sessions and in specialized schools such as the Nguyen Ai Quoc School in Hanoi (supervised directly by Truong Chinh). As much as 10 percent of the entire cadre corps may be in Party schools at any one time.

Le Duan, who has written extensively over the years about the cadre system, lists as important qualities: loyalty to communism and to Party lines and policies, leadership ability, identification with the proletariat, strong sense of organization and organizational discipline, competence in fulfilling duties, ideological orientation and knowledge about Marxism-Leninism, and a stable, determined personality. Le Duan has described the cadre as the chief institution in implementing Party/state programs. The cadre, by the fact of his personality, shapes his organization; therefore, the organization becomes a manifestation of cadre behavior, an extension of the cadre himself. The truly successful cadre masters organizational techniques and the uses of social institutions and then marries organizational activity to ideology. Le Duan has stressed that there must be no activity independent from ideology, that all activity must be explainable in ideological terms, and that to do so is the central task of the cadre.

Such is the ideal. Obviously, the number of individuals turned up by genetic accident with these superhuman qualities is limited in any society. Rare indeed is the individual who can walk into a meeting and deliver a speech that brings people to their feet shouting, who can then organize efficiently some complex agricultural production task or (if in the South) lay a faultless ambush of an enemy military convoy. Further, by the nature of his work—communicating a personalized message tailored to a particular need at a particular moment—cadre impact, however great, is restricted to a small circle of individuals. The cadre in no way is a mass medium. Finally, the mortality rate among good cadres during the crucial wartime years was extremely high. Being dedicated, they took the greatest risks and consequently suffered the highest toll. No one has been more outspoken on the subject of cadre quality than has Le Duan. In a remarkably candid late 1974 speech, he declared that only

30 to 40 percent of all Party cadres could be considered "active" that is, energetic and diligent. Another 40 percent, he said, was only "middling," doing just enough to get by. He dismissed the remaining 10 to 20 percent as "no good."

Party cadre quality was at its zenith during the Viet Minh War and has gone downhill steadily ever since. The most common complaints about cadres, as gleaned from Hanoi press reports over the years, are: laziness, corruption, lack of leadership ability, ignorance of Party policies (and changes in policies), and indifference to ideology. With innate ability rare, training time long, and attrition rate high, the Party has suffered a permanent shortage of quality cadres and has been forced to accept the mediocre or inadequate. Insufficiency of good cadres is the chief weakness in the entire system.

Whatever its shortcomings, however, the cadre system does work. It provides the necessary connection between the individual and the vast, vague thing known as the Party/state. It profitably harnesses youthful energies, either to change or to perpetuate the social order. It is an antidote for the alienation suffered by the individual in the uncaring modern-day mass society. It is a means of setting and maintaining high uniform standards of behavior, both personal and professional, for a key segment of the society, thus offering the young, in particular, a model of behavior within the system that is idealistic and yet allows for honors, status, influence, and all the other rewards the system has to bestow. If any single factor can explain Party success over the years, the cadre system comes closest.

Chapter 5

Viet Minh War: Crucible Years

More than any other single factor, the Viet Minh War is responsible for what the Lao Dong Party and the new Socialist Republic of Vietnam are today. In the fire of what was widely seen as a holy war, whose essence was spirit, was forged the character of today's Vietnamese Communist. Events then set Vietnam on a course that still is not run today. The social trauma of that period will continue to dominate both Party and state as long as the present generation of leaders lives.

The period began in early 1946 with an initial Party power play amidst a momentary truce with the French; it ended in Geneva in the summer of 1954. It was a time filled with decisive events, unexpected developments, and historical might-have-beens. The major ones:

* The Party consolidated its power and outmaneuvered, then broke the back of, its non-Communist opposition.

* Negotiation efforts by the French to make some workable political arrangement were initiated early, pursued haphazardly, and ended in failure.

* Military combat was fierce and bitter, the fortunes of war on both sides fluctuating widely; eventually the Viet Minh strategy of protracted conflict proved to the correct one, for the French lost heart and quit.

* Victory by the Communists in China raised the Viet Minh War from a regional struggle to an international problem.

* The Lao Dong Party was created, its cadre apparatus developed, its ideological orientation fixed, and its leadership structure created.

* The governing administrative arrangement—a troika of Party, government (DRV), and mass organization (Viet Minh/Lien Viet), with the Party monopolizing power—began creating new economic institutions, political patterns, and social relationships.

The question of war—whether it could be avoided, when it would come—dominated the months immediately following the August Revolution. There was a struggle for power within a condition of anarchy. There were some killings, especially in Saigon, and small-scale skirmishes with the French. In October 1945 a truce was effected. The initial Viet Minh governing arrangement in Hanoi—sixteen cabinet posts, of which six were held by members of the ICP—was unsatisfactory to the occupying Chinese as well as to the French, to whom the Chinese in effect turned over occupation rights, as did the British in the South. The result was a new government, officially termed the Government of National Union and Resistance. It consisted of twelve ministries, two of which were held by ICP members, and its National Assembly met for its first session in March 1946. The assembly quickly became a rubber stamp; within a year the number of official opposition had dropped from seventy to two. Ho Chi Minh unveiled a new constitution on November 9, 1946. The same month, the National Assembly met and officially created the Mat Tran Lien Hiep Quoc Dan Viet Nam (United Vietnam Nationalist Front), or Lien Viet, as the new broadest possible united front.[1]

France had announced, after its forces returned to Indochina, that it was willing to see Indochina become a locally autonomous federation within the French Union. Negotiations followed, and in March 1946 a preliminary Franco–Viet Minh agreement was signed. It called for a halt to bloodshed; the establishment of the Republic of Vietnam with its own government, legislature, budget, and armed forces, but as part of the French Union (and within the Federation of Indochina); the stationing of 15,000 French troops in Vietnam; a referendum on unification of the three regions of Vietnam; and subsequent negotiations to work out details and settle other existing issues.

The arrangement might have worked, at least for an interim period. While much was cloudy about the notion of membership in the French

Union, the sense of it was that the Vietnamese would have self-determination in a unified Vietnam. But this meant a loss of French status, unacceptable to the French *colon*. Powerful both in Indochina and in Paris, the *colon*, in the end, was able to sabotage the agreement. Had a stronger government existed in Paris, the *colon* might have been resisted. Also the sense of the agreement was that the French would continue to have a privileged economic position in Indochina, which, in the long run at least, was unacceptable to the Vietnamese. Thus *colon* machismo and economic contradictions dimmed, but did not necessarily doom, hope for an evolutionary arrangement satisfactory to both French and Vietnamese.

The summer of 1946 was marked by maneuver. The Fontainebleau Conference (July 1946), which was to write a formal Franco-Vietnamese agreement, ended inconclusively. The French continued to build up their forces. The Viet Minh were occupied with internal opposition. In November, fighting broke out in Haiphong over the issue of customs control and ended with French bombardment of portions of the city. The Viet Minh government began moving out of Hanoi. On December 19, 1946—the date DRV historians give as the start of the war—Viet Minh forces simultaneously struck several French positions in Hanoi and across Tonkin in what the French regarded as a sneak attack, ending in a massacre of French civilians (40 civilians were killed, 171 wounded, and 169 abducted). The war had begun.

WAR: COURSE AND STRATEGY

The early years witnessed a war of movement and position. The Viet Minh fought defensively, preventing French village-level rule and preventing peace, but unable to win. In 1947 the Viet Minh's strategic position began to improve. Its forces fanned out across the countryside to provide a screen behind which cadres organized villagers into revolutionary committees and local guerrilla bands. The French retired to strong points and began systematic development of their forces. They seized the initiative in late 1947 in a China border campaign designed to block outside arms traffic. The operation was inconclusive and served to foster an attitude that had been developing on both sides for some months—that the war was destined to become an endless, even if dynamic, standoff, one in which the Viet Minh were too well located and too widely supported ever to be decisively defeated given existing French military limitations and political conditions in France, but also one in which inherent Viet Minh weakness, particularly in terms of firepower, meant the Viet Minh could not put together the force necessary to end French control of urban areas and lines of communication.

Communist victory in China, in late 1949, changed the Indochinese situation profoundly, making Viet Minh victory possible if not probable. A Viet Minh offensive in 1950 forced the French out of the Sino-Vietnamese border region, facilitating the flow of Chinese Communist aid, mainly arms and training cadres. By 1954 aid had reached the level of 4,000 tons per month; Chinese military personnel, as advisors and technicians, numbered about 8,000.[2] Much less aid came from the USSR, partly because of transportation difficulties. Significant also was the lack of support from the French Communist Party which, at the time the war began, had hopes of achieving political power in France and did not want to alienate Frenchmen unnecessarily. Hence, French Communist Party chief Maurice Thorez was quoted as saying that under no circumstance did the French Communist Party wish to liquidate the French position in Indochina.[3]

Major battles were fought in the northern part of the country during the 1947–48 autumn-winter campaign, the 1948–49 winter-spring campaign, and the 1950 border campaign. The southern part of the country—that is, Annam and Cochin China, what were called Viet Minh Zones Five and Six—was less strategically important than Tonkin (80 percent of the Viet Minh forces were north of Vinh) and was regarded mostly as a source of manpower and supply rather than as a theatre of operations.

The year 1951 was a bad one for the Viet Minh, its forces suffering several important reverses. That same year the Party's Second Congress met and ordered intensified warfare, resulting in a major campaign, generally successful, in the northern part of the Red River Delta in late 1951. Gradually the tide began to turn. Increasingly, the Viet Minh was able to launch offensives: into Laos in 1952 and 1953, then into southern Vietnam and Cambodia, and then again into Laos in 1954. The thrust toward Laos triggered a French blocking operation, using a base built at Dien Bien Phu. The base became a gauntlet thrown down by the French and picked up by the Viet Minh. Dien Bien Phu was a classic thirteenth-century seige battle. It was won stunningly and surprisingly by the Viet Minh, largely because their forces were able to haul artillery pieces through the mountains, something judged impossible by French intelligence. The base surrendered on May 8, 1954, marking the end of the Viet Minh War. Hostilities were officially terminated ten weeks later.[4]

In many respects the Viet Minh War—or the Resistance, as the Viet Minh termed it—was something new on the world's military scene. It is described by many terms, *people's war* perhaps being the best if used in the technical sense of people employed as the instrument of war. It borrowed much from the Chinese Communist revolution and, in fact, extended and refined the Maoist strategy. Its two elements were armed struggle and political struggle, the first involving guerrilla and main-force warfare as well as assassinations and kidnappings; the second, intensive organizational and motivational efforts among Vietnamese villagers, with the entire conflict set in the context of a protracted struggle. It was very much a logistics war, at which General Giap proved to be exceptionally adept. Finally, it was marked by what was to become famous as the fighting-negotiating gambit: a series of political settlement proposals by one side and then the other, with neither acting in much faith or even interest.

For their part, the French tried to fight a traditional kind of war and at the same time find an alternative to the Viet Minh. After three years of lost time they settled on a governing arrangement headed by the emperor Bao Dai, but it had no success.

Postwar Party histories make the Party central to all activity during the Viet Minh War. For example:

> In early 1953, based on a scientific analysis of the battlefield situation throughout Indochina, the Party's Central Committee set forth the strategic precept for the 1953–54 Winter-Spring campaign. . . .
> In December 1953, the Party Central Committee decided to conduct a strategic battle at Dien Bien Phu. . . . The strategic determination of the Central Committee was quickly converted into the will and action of the entire Party and Army. . . .
> At the time of the great [Dien Bien Phu] victory the Party Central Committee, holding its Sixth Conference (July 1954), unanimously agreed with the Political Bureau on the decision to negotiate. . . .
> The great war victory . . . was the result of the valiant armed struggle of the Vietnamese people under the leadership of the Party and President Ho. . . .[5]

ORGANIZATION BUILDING

The crucible years of war shaped the Party, organizationally and intellectually, into a form that remains paramount to this day. It has several hallmarks: a premium on organizational work over all other activity; intensive use of a monopolistic communication system that raises to a high art the practice of various motivation, agitation, propaganda, and emulation programs; and collective decision making that institutionalizes doctrinal disputes and thus reduces the chance of bloody power struggle or the need for internal purges.

The system was created largely in the year and a half between the power seizure attempt of the August Revolution and the beginning of the war when the DRV/Viet Minh were driven from Hanoi and established both government and operational base in the mountainous regions to the Northwest. The organization was a triad of Party, government, and mass, or front, groups—the three components that were then, as they are today, the basic building blocks of the Vietnamese communist society.

To court Vietnamese who were anti-French but suspicious of communism, the ICP Central Committee announced on November 11, 1945, that in the name of national unity the Indochinese Communist Party had been dissolved. There would remain, it added, only a Marxist Study Association, presumably a small band of intellectuals interested in theoretical discussions.[6] For the next five years, officially and publicly, there was no communist party in Vietnam. In fact, however, Party recruitment continued, Party leadership activities went on as usual, and high-level (but not lower-echelon) congresses were staged: a Party plenum two months later, an enlarged Party Central Committee session at Huong Canh in March 1946, the very important First Cadre Conference in Ha Dong in July 1946, and other meetings of similar importance held regularly. All of this later was officially chronicled by Truong Chinh himself.

The Party not only grew during its time of dissolution but became bloated. Membership at the time of the August Revolution was about 5,000. In the subsequent fifteen-month consolidation period it rose to 15,000 and by the time the Lao Dong Party was formed in 1951 it stood at 700,000. This rapid, indiscriminate expansion violated the Leninist principle of the party as the small, elite vanguard of the vanguard. It admitted to membership persons of questionable background as well as a considerable number of incompetents and opportunists. And, inevitably, it created ill will, factionalism, and power struggles between the old guard and the more numerous newcomers. Rapid growth combined with the official state of nonexistence had a secondary effect. It reduced interaction between the leadership and the rank and file, lessening even the previous modest influence of the ordinary member, which could be exerted through Party meetings, regional conferences, and Party congresses. The nature of power within the Vietnamese communist movement during this period was monopoly without redeeming panoply, a pattern that would endure and prove to be both strength and weakness.

Party documents of the era indicate that considerable dissatisfaction with the organizational structure existed among the top leadership. A January 1948 plenum devoted itself mainly to what were called irregularities in Party development, such as independent initiatives by basic Party units, admission to membership (even promotion to positions of power) of persons with exploiter/reactionary backgrounds, failure of cadres to maintain proper standards of discipline, and, in general, a decline in the quality of cadre and member alike. The plenum's overall assessment was that Party organizational work was fairly good in Tonkin, poor in Annam, and almost nonexistent in Cochin China. Concern was also shown for counterorganizational activity by the French.

Throughout the Viet Minh War the Party pursued its organizational work with the twin basic purposes of controlling the disparate anti-French elements that made up the Viet Minh and increasing its strength relative to the Nationalists within and outside the Viet Minh. This involved three major activities: (a) redesigning the Party-front relationship, (b) political maneuvering to undercut French political gestures among the Vietnamese, and (c) elimination, including physical destruction where necessary, of opposition to Party control and management of the war.

The vortex of this three-way struggle was the Viet Minh, which began the war with a claimed 500,000 members (200,000 in Tonkin and 150,000 each in Annam and Cochin China), plus another 500,000 active supporters. Within the Viet Minh, its ideology camouflaged by Nationalist banners, the Party sought to outorganize, outrecruit, and outproselyte all internal opposition. Always, of course, the Party was numerically in the minority. For several years the arrangement served the Party well, but gradually the communist connection became too obvious and the Viet Minh image began to tarnish. So Ho Chi Minh, master organization man that he was, decided to drown the Viet Minh in a still larger front organization, the Lien Viet. It was to be less politicized and would include religious organizations and other nonpolitical groups; in fact, it would include any element that agreed the French should be expelled. The Lien Viet was billed as *the* transnational patriotic organization that should appeal to all Vietnamese except traitors.

The new, broader front organization proved to pose no problem of control for Ho and the Party. In fact, a new law of organizations was being worked out: the larger an organization, the easier for a small group to manage it. The Lien Viet was headed by Ton Duc Thang, who later would become president of the DRV. Its Central Committee was composed of twelve Party members, six Viet Minh/Party collaborators, and nine others. Its apparat, to the extent it existed, was composed almost entirely of Party cadres, well trained by Ho in the techniques of organizational infighting. The Viet Minh was not abolished; rather, it continued to exist within the Lien Viet although in a highly ambiguous relationship. The restructuring provided for the Party an arena in which it could outmaneuver its political rivals and consolidate its power among the rank and file. This is not to say the Lien Viet/Viet Minh arrangement was always a manipulative fraud. For a time—until 1950—it was a genuine coalition in which the Party shared political power.

This organizational victory deeply impressed Party leaders and conditioned Party thinking about the proper management of political opposition. The lesson was clear: make less use of naked force and more use of organizational, motivational, and communication-control mechanisms.

The Lien Viet shifted anti-French politics somewhat to the left, a fact that probably bothered few Vietnamese at the time. The Viet Minh's single objective had been emancipation (usually expressed in the context of self-determination), while the Lien Viet proclaimed two themes, anti-imperialism and antifeudalism. The two were treated with equal importance. This was a significant change. Antifeudalism had an important economic dimension, which was apparently dictated by internal Party needs but which at the time went largely unnoticed.

With the mass organizations as the base, a government, or at least an administrative system, was created that allowed effective control of much of the countryside despite the presence of a large French army. This administration duplicated the Franco-Vietnamese district/village-level administration with a clandestine authority, what the French called parallel hierarchies. In the Viet Minh, or Liberated, zone in the early days, Party control was informal, as was the organizational structure itself. Villages were administered by a resistance committee, or administrative committee (*uy ban hanh chinh xa*), guided by local or imported Party cadres. The five-man committee consisted of a president, a vice president for security, a secretary handling paperwork, one member handling finances, and one responsible for public works and mutual-aid agricultural operations. Often the village also contained a guerrilla unit led by a village committee vice president for self-defense. Above the village was the *lien xa*, the intervillage group. Next was the *huyen*, or district committee, called Uy Ban Khang Chien Hanh Chinh, the Committee for Resistance and Administration. Later its military tasks were divorced from it, and it became simply an administrative committee.

The three elements above the district—the *tinh* (province), the *khu* (zone), and the *lien khu* (interzone)—were essentially military command structures, not civil administrations. The *khu*, fourteen in all of Vietnam, was a group of provinces commanded by the equivalent of a general (later in the war the *khu*, or zone, level was eliminated). The *lien khu* was the highest administrative level. There were six of these: One and Two were the mountainous regions of Tonkin; Three, the Red River Delta; Four and Five, northern and southern Annam; and Six, Cochin China. As a separate military command there was the Left Bank, the northern stretch of the Red River Delta extending to the mountainous zones.[7]

The armed forces, created by General Giap early in World War II, were redesigned under Chinese guidance into a main force and a guerrilla force. A Party political commissar system was developed to insure Party control of the military.

Within the Viet Minh/DRV–controlled area, no political opposition could legally exist, nor was there any parliamentary opposition in the DRV National Assembly after 1946. Certain groups, officially termed nonpolitical, remained organizationally coherent, mainly the Buddhists (as the National Buddhist Association), the Cao Dai element (termed Twelve United Sects), and some of the Catholics of northern Vietnam (in two organizations, the National Salvation Catholic League and the National Liaison Committee of Patriotic and Peace-Loving Catholics). In addition, there were Viet Minh area-wide organizations of women, youth, students, farmers, and intellectuals. A Vietnam Peace Committee did liaison work with sympathetic groups abroad. None of these organizations had much administrative control. Policy determination, as well as the more important operational offices in the DRV, was in the hands of Party members. Specific elements charged with insuring conformity were the cong an, or secret police, the trinh sat, or military intelligence, and the dich van, squads responsible for "moral intervention," that is, psychological warfare and the use of violence for psychological purposes.

Outside the Viet Minh zone, political maneuvering sought to undercut those Vietnamese attempting to deal with the French. The then-existing Government of Vietnam was shattered through various disorganizational techniques, its top officials—such as the vice president and foreign minister—forced to flee to China to join the government's nominal chief, Bao Dai. In 1949, after two years of negotiating, the French persuaded Bao Dai to return to Vietnam as chief of what was to be an independent Government of Vietnam within the French Union. The organizational struggle between this government and the DRV/Viet Minh continued throughout the war.

In addition to restructuring the front organization and countering Franco-Vietnamese collaboration, the Party was involved in a third organizational struggle. This was a campaign of destruction aimed at its various enemies: the Trotskyists (Ta Thu Thau), the sectarian groups, the smaller moderate political groups (the Constitutional Party, the Independence Party, the Dong Minh Hoi), and, most of all, its two old rivals, the Dai Viet and the VNQDD.

This campaign to emasculate the Nationalists, as the VNQDD was to describe it later, began with the return of the Viet Minh and the Party to Hanoi after World War II. It lasted for about a year and a half, reaching its most brutal level in the months following June 1946, when the last of the KMT troops departed Vietnam. For a year and a half, Viet Minh police and troops hunted down leaders and important members of the VNQDD, Dai Viet, Dong Minh Hoi, and Trotskyist movement. Publications were shut down. Leaders were assassinated, including Ta Thu Thau in Quang Ngai, Pham Quynh in Hue, and Bui Quang Chieu outside Saigon. Vo Hong Khanh returned from China in 1945 to take a ministerial post in the new government, only to flee again. Members were scattered. The Dai Viets were driven south from Hanoi, chiefly to the

Hue-Danang region of central Vietnam. There, they trained members in guerrilla war techniques, operated a radio station, and fought for years against the Viet Minh, the French, and later the newly formed government of Ngo Dinh Diem.[8]

The main target, of course, was the VNQDD, whose leaders had returned to Hanoi on the heels of the occupying Nationalist Chinese forces. The VNQDD, as noted earlier, advocated emancipation from the French and a republican form of government for Vietnam. An early member of the Viet Minh, the VNQDD was purged in 1946, after which a bitter struggle began, often marked by pitched battles in the villages around Hanoi. The Viet Minh/Party rationale for the campaign against the VNQDD was that it must be eliminated for attempting to sabotage the truce that had been established—which the VNQDD was in fact doing in assassinating Frenchmen, blowing up French outposts, and raiding French installations to capture arms and ammunition. General Giap's forces, aided by the French in some instances, attacked VNQDD offices and population centers in Hanoi, Lang Son, Haiphong, and the Hon Gay area as guerrilla fought guerrilla. For fifteen months something of a three-sided war was fought among the French, Viet Minh, and VNQDD, with the first two allied against the third and emerging as the only survivors.[9]

By late 1947 the Party's organizational cadres and General Giap's more direct methods had completed the task. All organized Viet Minh opposition to the idea of collaboration with the Party had been eliminated. All effective anti-French activity by Nationalists outside the Viet Minh had been smashed. All opposing organizations within the Franco-Vietnamese sphere were in ruins at the village level and only a hollow shell at the center. The Viet Minh alone carried the banners of nationalism against the French, and the central force within the Viet Minh was the Party.

The 1940s saw the emergence of several new Party figures, including:

* Chu Van Tan (b. 1908, Thai Nguyen province), a Nung who began Party activities in the mid-1930s and led guerrilla forces against the Japanese during World War II. He held important command assignments during the Viet Minh War, later was involved in Party work among the military and in ethnic minority affairs.

* Do Muoi (b. 1917, Hanoi), the most capable manager of industrial/ construction activities at the Central Committee level. A political commissar during the Viet Minh War, he switched to the DRV economic sector in 1955 and became a ramrod for domestic construction although both he and his work became eclipsed by the Vietnam War.

* Xuan Thuy (b. 1912, Hanoi), son of a Confucian scholar and an early activist. He became one of the Party's chief agitprop cadres during the Viet Minh War, later switching to foreign affairs. Named foreign minister in 1963, then removed two years later for reasons never made clear, he led the DRV delegation at the Paris talks beginning in 1968.

* Tran Dang Khoa (b. 1907, Hue), one of the most influential of the Party technocrats. A civil engineer, Khoa for thirty years has directed DRV public works, chiefly in rural areas where water conservation projects are the major task.

LAO DONG FORMATION

As we have seen, the Vietnamese communist movement grew steadily in size and strength during the last half of the 1940s. Gradually it emerged from its official state of nonexistence. With a membership of nearly three-quarters of a million in a country of only fifteen million adults, it could hardly be otherwise.

In January 1950 an ICP conference (the term *ICP* still was used internally) convened to address itself to the matter of formal status. It was part of a more fundamental question of when and under what circumstances the Party was to assume a monopoly of power in the Lien Viet/Viet Minh structure. The decision was made to re-form and resurface as an orthodox communist party.

The Second Party Congress, later called the Resistance War Congress, convened February 11–19, 1951, at Vinh Quang in Tuyen Quang province, chaired by Ho Chi Minh and attended by 211 delegates (158, plus 52 alternates) as well as by observers from the Chinese and Siam Communist parties. The Dang Lao Dong Vietnam, or Vietnamese Workers Party, was inaugurated with Ho as chairman and Truong

Chinh as secretary general. The congress elected a new Central Committee and Politburo, approved an amended set of bylaws (which lowered the age for entrance to the Party from twenty-three to eighteen), established a new Control Committee, and authorized the establishment of a Party newspaper, *Nhan dan* (the first edition of which, as a weekly, appeared March 11, 1951). Membership was reported as 728,211. The following month, on March 3, 1951, the Lao Dong Party was formally presented to the world.

Emergence of the Lao Dong Party had several implications for the Vietnamese situation.

* It marked the beginning of the "regularization" of Party-front relations, that is, conversion of the Lien Viet/Viet Minh from a genuine power-sharing collaboration between party and nonparty to an instrument of Party interest.

* It made respectable, at least legal, that which had been secret and, in a sense, illegitimate. The Party was known by all to exist—a pregnant woman does not easily pass unnoticed, a Party historian dryly wrote at the time—and thus its emergence, particularly when labeled a workers party, was both corrective and an adjustment to reality. The official rationale was that the time had come for the Party to provide full and open leadership in pressing toward final victory in the war and inaugurating national construction along socialist lines, and for this the Party needed a more legitimate image. The status change, however, was largely a matter of degree. A 1951 Party instruction noted:

> Although appearing officially and announcing its views and policies the Party will not necessarily reveal its organization. . . . There is no question of exposing the entire Party membership indiscriminately. A certain number of representative comrades, those well trained and well regarded, will be chosen to represent the Party officially.[10]

* It permitted a clearer division of labor between covert and overt work, the former now confined to the Party and latter becoming the nearly exclusive concern of the mass, or front, organization complex that was streamlined and reemphasized in March 1951 at the Congress of Unification of the Lien Viet and Viet Minh fronts.

* It established the ground for internal Party overhaul. Following the Second Congess, Party recruitment was virtually halted for nearly two years. Recent recruits were subjected to an intensive reindoctrination course. Perhaps as many as 5 percent of all members were deemed unreliable or incompetent and dropped from the rolls. The internal Party chain of command—interzone, province, district, village/block, cell—remained essentially the same. The Party Central Committee (nineteen members, ten alternates) subsequently expanded to create a Political Bureau, or Politburo, and a Party Control Section. The focus here was on Tonkin. Administrative affairs in the South, what had been the Nam Bo Party Regional Committee area, were vested in a six-man Central Office of South Vietnam, which at first was an appendage of the Central Committee and later became more formalized as the Southern Branch of the Lao Dong Party.

* It permitted, or required, a more precise statement of what the Party stood for and what was meant by communism in Vietnam. No longer was it possible or necessary to explain all actions and beliefs in vague terms of national spirit or antifeudalism. In a sense, it can be said that Vietnamese communist ideology was invented in 1951, because for the first time there appeared a systematic and consistent interpretation of historical phenomena in Marxist terms. Out of the Second Congress came statements directed at the rank and file and explaining what was unique about the Party. "The *Lao Dong* Party was built on and guided by the doctrinal thoughts of Marx, Engels, Lenin and Mao Tse-tung." (Note the absence of Stalin.) The Party's mission in Vietnam was listed as threefold: "To eliminate the invading imperialists, to suppress remaining feudal and semi-feudal ruling elements, and to achieve the goal of 'to each his own land.' "[11] Party organization, it was stated, rests on iron discipline and democratic centralism. Training of Party members requires *kiem thao* ("criticism and self-criticism") sessions. The Party has the duty of aiding revolutionary movements in Cambodia and Laos as well as antiimperialist forces in Malaya, Indonesia, Burma, and elsewhere in Southeast Asia.

* It helped internationalize the Party and integrate it into the worldwide Communist movement as an orthodox element. Joining the international mainstream was given as the reason for dropping the name *Indochina* in favor of *Vietnam,* as well as the use of *worker* instead of *communist,* asserted to be ideologically fashionable.[12]

* It enabled an organizational spin-off by the Cambodian and Lao
  Communist parties, ending the old, unwieldy arrangement in favor
  of one more appropriate to current operating conditions. The argument presented to cadres on this issue was that the character of the
  struggle and the indigenous social conditions in Laos and Cambodia
  varied so widely from Vietnam that separate party structures were
  required. Implicit in this argument was the assertion that the idea of a
  single party for all of Indochina (as fixed in 1930) had been forced on
  local comrades by the Comintern. Throughout the war, the Party and
  the Viet Minh assisted and guided the anti-French struggle by the Lao
  and Cambodians, although the war in their countries was but a pale
  reflection of the one raging in northern Vietnam.

* It fixed as Vietnam's main socioeconomic issue the question of land
  tenure, involving various agrarian programs, land redistribution, and
  land-reform projects. Thus, a connection between land and the anti-
  French struggle was established. Where able, Party cadres seized land
  from French nationals or Vietnamese collaborators and distributed it
  to the landless. Lower land-rental rates were established and enforced
  by Viet Minh guerrillas. The purpose of this, said the Party, was to
  transfer political power from landowner to peasant, and any economic
  benefits derived could be justified only in terms of contribution to
  the struggle. The Lao Dong manifesto on land holdings decreed that
  only "peasants who are production fighters . . . shall benefit from the
  reduction in land rent, interest rates and agrarian reform." In 1951
  land tenure became one of the two major Party concerns (the other
  being Party leadership over war strategy) and was later officially
  described thus:

> In the process of carrying out the mission of liberating our people,
> the Party also managed to carry out its anti-feudal mission step by step
> such as: redistribution of public land and rice plantations, distribution
> to the people of lands belonging to the colonialists and their henchmen,
> decrease of land rental and profit rates. By 1953 the Party was already
> able to launch the peasants on a land reform campaign in the areas
> where conditions permitted.[13]

All of this last eventually became part of what was called the economic
leveling campaign, that is, the systematic ruin of the landholding farmer,
the urban businessman, and the Vietnamese middle class. In its full

fruition it became, not an economic program at all, but an effort to alter basic social relationships. This ambitious and far-reaching program is considered later in this chapter.

GENEVA, 1954

Beginning in 1951—after the Chinese Communist victory—the Viet Minh War increasingly was seen abroad, not as a local conflict, but as an international problem. Interest and pressure developed to settle at the conference table. French failure to achieve victory in the field and growing political disarray in France finally brought to power a government committed to ending the war. For its part, the Party became increasingly interested in a settlement. It was weaker and more exhausted than the world realized. It was under pressure from the USSR (interested in making a trade with the French—peace in exchange for French scuttling of the European Defense Community) as well as from the PRC (at the moment pursuing its benign foreign policy laid out at the Bandung Conference). Party leaders wanted to legitimize what they had won and were willing to pay a certain price for this. The leadership feared (or professed that it feared) intervention by the United States or SEATO forces. Finally, the Party and DRV leaders were convinced that even a settlement based on partition, with a southern party of Vietnam in the hands of Ngo Dinh Diem, would collapse of its own weight within a few months.

All of these pressures developed and combined to make possible for the first time a negotiated end to the fighting. On the initiative of Britain, France, and the United States at a foreign ministers' conference with the USSR in Berlin in February 1954, it was agreed to stage a conference in Geneva to which interested parties would be invited to discuss the situation in Korea, where a cease-fire had been arranged the previous July, and in Indochina. The Geneva Conference on Korea and Indochina opened in late April of 1954, taking up first the question of Korea. When a deadlock was reached, the United States formally withdrew and John Foster Dulles went home, leaving an observer team behind to attend the second part of the conference, to begin May 8, on Indochina. The participants were Britain and the USSR as cohosts; the French, representing both themselves and Bao Dai's state of Vietnam;

the Democratic Republic of Vietnam; the kingdoms of Laos and Cambodia; and the People's Republic of China. The Republic of Vietnam, in which Bao Dai soon was to be deposed by referendum in favor of Ngo Dinh Diem, did not attend and in fact denounced the whole affair.

On July 20 a cease-fire agreement was initialed by French and Viet Minh generals. The following day a Final Declaration was issued. It was not signed by anyone. The United States issued a statement acknowledging the Final Declaration and agreeing not to act by force so as to upset it (with the clear implication that if someone else upset it by force the United States would be free to act in any way it saw fit).

The essence of the Geneva Accords was that it freed the French from a trap of their own creation and permitted them to walk away from Indochina with a certain amount of dignity. A cease-fire was arranged, and Vietnam was temporarily divided to permit the separation of the contending forces. Nothing was settled with respect to the political future of the country. Quite the contrary. All political problems were swept under the rug with a vague call in the Final Declaration for elections, although without stating what kind of elections or to what specific political purpose.[14] At the time, the failure to fix future political arrangements was not considered by most Party officials to be particularly serious. They believed—and were told by their allies—that they had won all of Vietnam, that it was simply a matter of waiting a few months for the remaining opposition, chiefly Diem in Saigon, to disintegrate.

Some Party leaders and cadres in Hanoi were less enthusiastic, viewing the Geneva Conference as a victory, but a qualified victory. A few officials, among them Le Duan, who did not go to Geneva, were barely able to conceal their hostility. Western journalists in Hanoi say Le Duan and other ranking Party members bluntly told them during the conference that the Vietnam cause was being betrayed, and once it had ended they expressed forebodings about the future.

CONCLUSIONS ON THE CRUCIBLE YEARS

Several important judgments can be offered about the years between the time of the Party's formation in 1930 and its coming to power in 1954.

The two most important developments were the military/psychological defeat of the French and the 1950 ICP decision to change the structure of the resistance from what it was—an authentic coalition of Communists and Nationalists actually sharing power—to complete and overt assumption of control by the ICP.

The period itself was something of a classic example of communist developmental progression: (a) form the party with a proletarian base to act as vanguard (and by revolutionary metamorphosis convert the middle and intellectual classes into proletarians); (b) form a united-front alliance to challenge the ruling group (the French and the French collaborators); (c) fight a people's war using armed and political struggle in protracted conflict; and (d) establish a people's republic.

The Viet Minh was, or became, the only significant Vietnamese nationalist vehicle during this all-important period, the one transnational organization with significant outside connections and support. Nationalists outside the Viet Minh lacked organization, leadership, cohesion, doctrinal focus—in short, were deficient in every major sector.

The Party skillfully dominated the Viet Minh and through it the struggle against the French. In doing so, the Communists could lead, but not push. They succeeded in establishing operational control mainly because of their superior organizational skills, because they made credible their assertions of common interest, and because of default by non-Communist challengers. Party histories now usurp the anticolonial heritage, simplifying and equating all motivation with nationalism. That the Party was able to dominate the scene is doubly impressive in view of public opinion at the time. Attitudes of rank-and-file Viet Minh to the Party ranged from suspicious to hostile, particularly among Catholics and sect members. Popular support for the Viet Minh itself proved to be less extensive than even the French had believed. In the postwar Operation Exodus, which offered Vietnamese the opportunity to move in or out of the Viet Minh–controlled region, French planners anticipated transporting about 30,000 persons. The final figure was nearly one million, all but a fraction moving out and to the South. It became apparent afterward that nationalism had not polarized Vietnamese thinking and that in fact the largest single public opinion bloc was the famed Vietnamese *attentisme,* the fence-sitter waiting out the war to see who would win.

Political integration and the development of a modern governmental system by the DRV was facilitated immensely by the Viet Minh War. The newly formed DRV, under Ho Chi Minh, took on functions that no government in Vietnam had ever assumed in the past. It announced a territorial imperative: Vietnam is one. It pronounced a national identity, broader and more modern than the elemental, thousand-year Vietnamese ethnic consciousness. Indeed, Vietnamese identification formed the heart of the Viet Minh mystique and was mainly responsible for the defeat of the French. The war, of couse, made imperative the organizing of the Vietnamese population for the common purpose of emancipation. This meant, for the Vietnamese, a new definition of the relationship of government to governed. It altered traditional methods of allocating political power. It fixed new means of adjudicating disputes. It changed social relations. In short, it forced on a traditional society all of the changes involved in political development. But, and this is the point to be underscored, the problem of political integration that normally faces all new nations was minimized or buried in the transcendental trauma of the war. Normal political choice simply did not exist. Choice, to put it mildly, was polarized, even if opinion was not.

The DRV emerged from this forced development process as a modern state, crudely hewn perhaps, but with two to three decades compressed into five years. The new government, even though it was staking out a far larger sphere of activity than claimed by any previous one, found many of its problems of political integration already s Jlved. Catholics and other elements who would not be integrated had the option of moving out of the society, which many did.

The Party found the war to be of tremendous utility. Later, Party theoreticians would analyze the benefits and advantages derived from the war and would conclude, for the most part, that of the three basic elements involved in the Party's struggle to prevail—organization, strategy, and spirit—the first deserves major credit. Obviously, each was vital—victory would have been impossible without all three—but superior organization was what made the difference.

The cutting edge from the start had been spirit, the spirit of nationalism, of anticolonialism, of xenophobia, of *doc lap* with all of its unique overtones. In Marxism-Lenism the spirit found an ideological framework. For their part, the French lacked spirit. They needed Indochina economically, or so they believed, and there was a certain amount of empire building; but as spirit, this was a weak reed indeed. Non-Communist opposition—the Nationalists, later the Bao Dai government, and still later the Diem government—probably had about as much spirit as the Communists. What they lacked was effective organization. Constantly over the years they were outmaneuvered by the Communists, their positions in the villages undermined, their membership lists raided, the most promising young denied them by persuasive Party recruiters.

The French largely abandoned the psychological field to their enemies. The Viet Minh and the Party were able to arm themselves with the best rational and emotional arguments as to why the Vietnamese should oppose the French. They built a highly responsive machine, one that organized and energized the people and isolated the colonialists and all who would attempt to do business with them. The words *Viet Minh* and *patriotism* became virtually interchangeable.

But the Party's true genius, developed during these crucible years, was its ability to identify and then develop the great truths of organization. Some were insights by Ho Chi Minh, some were borrowed from the Chinese, some were the fruit of experience and experimentation.[15] Combined, they formed what amounted to a new discipline in sociology.

The great errors of the period, and the lessons learned from them by the Party, also were organizational. There were two major errors, both stemming from the 1951 decision fixing priorities. The first was the priority given to radical agrarian institutional change. This drained off enormous amounts of valuable cadre time and energy, to say nothing of popular support; it did, of course, serve to establish the Party as the dominant force. The second error was the order that concentrated Party building and rebuilding in the northern or Tonkin region while allowing the Southern Branch to drift along as best it could. This proved to be an historic strategic blunder. Party efforts in the South were limited and modest, mainly because there were so many difficulties both in Party building and in military and political operations. In retrospect, it is clear that the Party should have concentrated on this area so as to be prepared for the French departure. It could then have staged a second August Revolution, overpowering Ngo Dinh Diem and his weak, non-Communist, fragmented structure. When the opportunity presented itself, the Party could not capitalize on it.

Finally, the specific outcomes of the war—the Geneva Conference—and events that followed from it deeply prejudiced Party members and especially Party leaders against the general idea of negotiated settlements. They developed an almost reflexive distrust of the conference table. This was to have profound meaning for Vietnam two decades later.

Chapter 6

The Party in Power

The Viet Minh War had ended, and the hated French were driven out—that much had been settled by military force. But little else had been settled or even addressed. The people's hope for peace had been realized, but not their hopes for prosperity and political freedom.

The Party returned to Hanoi with a vengeance, not personal but social. Its power was great, nearly total, for all challenge to its authority had been destroyed, driven out, or discredited. Its ambition matched its power, ambition born of jungle dreams. Many were utopian dreams, never tested by reality but existing so long in the minds of the leaders that they gradually had become articles of faith. The Party returned wedded to an obsessive doctrine centered on the notion that social abstractions are more important than people. This was its orientation as it faced the host of pressing problems burdening the population: hunger, fear, unemployment, displacement, a ravaged agricultural sector, a distorted, war-shattered economy. It acted on the basis that only a communist system was appropriate for the DRV, that is, that the Party must monopolize political power, that all classes of the society must be reduced to one, that the economy must be industrial (rather than agrarian), and that politics is more important than economics in the sense that political control always overrides economic considerations such as productivity. The Party was not heartless. It cared about the sufferings of the people. But it cared more about the manner in which that suffering would be alleviated.

Social transformation of the society required extensive outside economic assistance, which, since the commitment was to communism, could come only from fellow socialist countries. That fact largely conditioned DRV external relations and behavior from 1954 onward.

Finally, the South had to be liberated and, by one means or another, the country united under a single communist banner.

These three goals, then—communization of the society, development of extensive outside sources of support, and unification of the fatherland—shaped the Party's future in the next two decades to the near exclusion of all else. The history of the Party after it came to power can be written in terms of these three goals.

CONSOLIDATION OF POWER

The first order of business was organizational overhaul of the society's three components—government, mass organization, and Party—made necessary by the transition from a jungle command directing a war to a capital-city government running a country. Consolidation of power began with reorganization and development of the country's military forces and internal security apparatus, required partly because of perceived threat—Diem in the South and counterrevolutionaries in the North—and partly because that was the Party way, to make armed and security forces central to the transformation of society.

The government, the Democratic Republic of Vietnam, was formally installed in Hanoi in October 1954. In theory, it continued to operate as it had in previous years, under its 1946 constitution. That document, however, had never been promulgated and, much later, was attacked by Party officials as being the work of traitors and therefore unprogressive. Administrative power, in name and fact, remained in the hands of the Party Central Committee. In 1960 the second constitution was promulgated and became the legal base of the government.[1]

In September 1955, following the Party's Eighth Plenum, the Lien Viet National Congress met and abolished itself, replaced by a new mass organization called the Vietnam Fatherland Front (Mat Tran To Quoc Viet Nam). Ho Chi Minh was elected honorary president and Ton Duc Thang vice president and principal officer. The Fatherland Front had two purposes: to be the principal mass movement in the DRV and to serve as the main operational element in the South. In the North it was conceived, not as a united front in the old sense, but as a transnational umbrella, incorporating not only the Lien Viet member organizations but the entire matrix of National Salvation Associations (Hoi Cuu Quoc). It came to serve many purposes. It sopped up the country's political energies, being the sole instrument by which candidates were and still are nominated and campaign in the periodic National Assembly elections. It is a centralized device for mobilizing the population in emulation campaigns and other outpourings of organized mass effort. It is a transmission belt for governmental information, explanations of Party policy, and other indoctrination work. It is a showcase for foreigners, an example of non-Party political power. It is the host organization for all private foreign visitors, those not being entertained officially by the Party or by the state.

The eighty-person Fatherland Front Executive Committee carefully draws members from all walks of life and includes numerous prominent non-Communist Vietnamese. The thirteen-person Presidium, however, is more exclusive, being composed mostly, if not entirely, of Party members.

Components of the Fatherland Front include: (a) the Lao Dong Party; (b) the Lao Dong Youth Group; (c) the Vietnam General Confederation of Trade Unions (500,000 members); (d) the Vietnam Democratic Party (organ of the remaining progressive bourgeoisie); (3) the Vietnam Socialist Party (organ of non-Communist progressive intellectuals); (f) the Vietnam Peace Committee, which, together with (g) the Vietnam Asian-African Solidarity Committee, deals with private outside political organizations; (h) the National Liaison Committee of Farmers; (i) the Vietnam Women's Union; (j) the Vietnam Writers and Artists Union; (k) the Vietnam Journalists Association; (l) the Industrialist and Trader Federation (superseded now by the Vietnam Chamber of Commerce); (m) the United Buddhist Association; and (n) the National Liaison Committee of Patriotic and Peace-Loving Catholics. Other organizations, some existing only in the South, are the Cao Dai and Hoa Hao sects, Montagnards, overseas Chinese, elderly villagers, and occupational specialists such as lawyers, doctors, and engineers. In all, the Fatherland Front is a mammoth organization of organizations, sweeping up virtually every social movement in the country. Its combined membership exceeds the country's adult population, since nearly every individual belongs to one or more Fatherland Front organizations.

In the South the initial concept of the Fatherland Front was orthodox, that is, a broad, irresistible, patriotic shield behind which the cause would advance. It inherited from the Lien Viet an extensive southern cell structure and for a period made overtures to various southern organizations seeking their membership or at least their cooperation. But it never became an effective instrument in the South. It continued to exist in a semimoribund state until replaced by the Vietnam National Liberation Front in 1960.

THIRD PARTY CONGRESS

The Party, upon its return to Hanoi in the post-Geneva period, became less ambiguous to the average citizen as far as its nature and role in society were concerned. But internally and organizationally it changed little, much less than did the state or the mass organizations. Top leadership at the time expressed considerable dissatisfaction with the lack of responsiveness by the Party organization and with the quality of cadres and members, but it confined its efforts to tinkering with the Party machinery. Much internal policy making involved deliberate delay, the decision to postpone taking action. Such was the case in convening the Third Congress. Originally scheduled for 1954, it was postponed yearly, until finally the leadership felt the time was ripe; and September 5–10, 1960, 576 members convened in Hanoi.

The major action of the congress was to announce and explain three new Party tasks or lines.

* Integrate the Party into the state's newly launched economic program of socialization. The essential need here was to insure Party primacy in fixing economic development theory and to maintain constant and total Party leadership in daily ongoing economic operations.

* Develop a strategy for the struggle in the South, that is, to achieve unification. This was seen as a multifaceted military-diplomatic task, involving mainly geopolitical or strategic considerations plus the development of sources of outside logistical support.

* Consolidate, and redefine to the degree necessary, the relationship of Party to society, particularly in terms of solving various social problems. This had both a negative and a positive dimension: destroy

those forces giving rise to counterrevolution on the one hand; and, on the other, purify and then enhance Party social control through what might be called a proto–cultural revolution.

The three tasks thus were economic, military, and social. For the next twenty-five years, transition to socialism, unification of the Fatherland, and the fostering of a social revolution in ideology and culture (as the three became sloganized) monopolized the lives of the people of the DRV. In like manner, the planning and guiding of these tasks, as well as the management of the doctrinal disputes that subsequently developed, dominated daily decision making by the top leadership.

Some organizational changes also emerged from the Third Congress. What was created has remained basically unchanged to this day. In brief, this organizational structure may be divided into three functional elements: the leadership, the intermediate cadre level, and the basic unit.

Party leadership consists of a Central Committee (forty-three regular, twenty-eight alternate members, plus some ten unannounced or "secret" members from the South); a Politburo (eleven members, two alternates), headed by a chairman and a first secretary[2] (Ho Chi Minh and Le Duan at the time). The chief staff element is a group of seventeen functional Central Committee departments dealing with: Party organization, defense, unification (war in the South), economic planning, propaganda and training, foreign relations, agriculture (rural affairs), industry, finance and trade, science and technological training, culture and education, emulation (motivation), doctrinal research, Party history, women's affairs, mass organization (Fatherland Front) affairs, and overseas Vietnamese affairs. There also are two specialized committees: the all-important Central Control Committee, which inspects and monitors all Party activity, and the Central Military Party Committee, which in turn is divided into two functional units, one handling Party organizational and administrative matters within the armed forces and the other responsible for supervising the political commissars found in all military units.

The cadre structure, that crucial element found between the leadership and the basic Party units, was changed little by the Third Congress, continuing to operate in the manner described earlier (see chapter 4).

At the bottom, or basic level, is the *chi bo*, the branch or chapter, which may be as small as three persons. The *chi bo* is broken down into three-person cells (*tieu to*).

Membership in the Party at the time of the Third Congress was about 525,000; in the Party Labor Youth Group, about 780,000; and in the Party Young Pioneers, about 600,000. Average Party age was fairly high, with some 80 percent of the membership having been on the rolls for more than ten years. The educational level was low—85 percent had less than four years' formal education—but this did not vary much from the national average. At least half of the estimated 110,000 key managers of the DRV economic system were Party members, a figure that was to rise steadily. Women comprised about 10 percent of the Party at the time of the Third Congress, a figure that doubled in the next five years. Under the recruiting drive that followed the congress, total membership rose to some 760,000 (according to Ho Chi Minh in April 1966) and then leveled off for a period at about 800,000. Most of the new recruits were young, hence the number of under-thirty members increased in five years from 39 to 81 percent. The recruiting was done at the expense of Party elitism, for the membership figure of the late 1960s represented 4.45 percent of the population. The drive also helped to make the Party proletarian. Of the 300,000 new members admitted after the 1960 congress, 50 percent were *ban co* ("landless poor"), 28 percent were middle peasants (i.e., lower-middle class), and 16 percent were workers. While this greatly changed the overall proletarian balance, the numbers had little effect at the upper level, where nonproletarians continued to dominate, even monopolize, positions of power. Virtually all of the 1960 Central Committee members were well-educated, experienced officials; about one-third of them were specialists in some field; and another third were what might be called educated generalists. Little new blood was added at the time to the top leadership. All of the Politburo members named at the congress had Party records dating back at least to the early 1930s; half of the Central Committee had been Party members since before World War II (Ho noted in a congress speech that thirty-one Central Committee members collectively had served a total of 222 years in French prisons). This small band of men would rule the DRV for the next decade and a half.

Three major documents came out of the Third Congress: new Party bylaws, a congress resolution, and a Party political report by Le Duan.

Collectively, these stressed, or reiterated:

* Marxism-Leninism must become more central in guiding all activity; increased indoctrination and training efforts must be launched to this end.

* Class consciousness must be reemphasized. There must be a deliberate effort to proletarianize the Party, making it more difficult for non-proletarians to enter.

* The Party, as vanguard of the proletarian dictatorship, must monopolize power and decision making at all levels.

* Organizationally, the Party must remain highly centralized, tightly hierarchical, and guided by the twin principles of democratic centralism and collective leadership.

* The chief Party enemies are individualism, rightist or leftist tendencies, and nonproletarian thought. The best defense against these is self-discipline.

For the Party in the South, the post-Geneva period obviously was a time of profound change. The first order of business was withdrawal of all threatened elements, and this was done during the regroupment effected by the Geneva Accords.[3] This effort was managed by a special organ, the Central Committee Directorate for the South (Trung Uong Cuc Mien Nam), which had been established in 1951 in the Camau Peninsula to coordinate Party affairs in the region.[4] It regrouped some 60,000 to 90,000 persons from South to North and ran Party affairs, such as they were, in the immediate post-Geneva period.

In mid-1954 the Politburo staged a southern cadre conference at which reorganization of the Southern Branch was outlined.

* The Party was to establish bases in the most secure of the old Viet Minh regions.

* It was to adopt the format of legal, semilegal, and illegal organizational structure.

* Membership ranks were to be purified, the undependable and incompetent weeded out (membership in two years dropped from 60,000 to 15,000). Those who were retained were to be reindoctrinated.

* Members should prepare for the advent of a new front organization, replacing the Lien Viet.

* Where possible, Party units should begin formation of self-defense groups, confining recruitment to the young, preferably teenagers.

* Southern Party affairs would continue to be handled by a mechanism outside normal Party channels. The Directorate would remain the supreme organ in the South. In Hanoi, a new Central Committee organ would be established, to be called the Central Unification Department and headed by Major General Nguyen Van Vinh. This department was to supervise the Party in the South and handle the affairs of the 50,000 or so southern regroupees earmarked for eventual return to the South.

Although statistics on the Party in the South are notoriously unreliable, it seems reasonably certain that at the time of the Geneva Accords there were about 130,000 loyalists in the South. Of these, 87,000 were military; 43,000, civilians. Of the total, about 60,000 were Party members, found both in military and civilian ranks. Nearly all of the 87,000 military plus some of the civilian loyalists were regrouped to the North, reducing southern Party membership. Further reduction occurred in the weeding-out process that followed and through defection to the Diem camp.[5] Thus, by the late 1950s the Party had about 15,000 members in the South, most of them civilians. The military strength it could claim—located in five ex–Viet Minh base areas—probably was not more than 3,000 or 4,000, although some historians place it as high as 10,000.

LAUNCHING SOCIALISM

The first of the two major tasks the Party set for itself at take-over, the second being unification, was conversion of the society to socialism/communism. This effort may be viewed in two dimensions, economic and noneconomic. The first is considered here and the second in a later section.

Under orthodox Marxism the historical stage following revolution should be capitalism. The Party in 1954 decided by a process of definition that it would skip the capitalist stage and proceed directly to construction

of socialism. This economic transition involved two goals: (a) transformation of the agricultural means of production, that is, collectivization, and (b) full and rapid heavy industrialization. In other words,
socialize what did exist and develop what did not. To this end it was
necessary to achieve two additional, implementing goals: (c) creation of a
state economic sector, replacing the market economy with a centrally
planned system, and (d) transformation of local industry—the handicraft
sector—into large, state-controlled enterprises.

The society inherited by the Party in 1954 had an ex-colonial agrarian
economy in which 90 percent of the labor force was engaged in feeding
the total population, a country with the least area of cultivated land per
inhabitant of any nation on earth. From the start, in purely economic
terms, planners faced a serious endemic agricultural problem: over-
population in a relatively small fertile area. Two-thirds of the DRV's
64,344 square miles was mountainous, and only about 5 percent of that
area was arable. Eighty percent of the population lived in the lowlands,
mainly in the Red River Delta, which had 75 percent of the population
and 75 percent of the arable land. The population in 1954 was estimated
at 12–13.5 million (92.6 percent rural, 7.4 percent urban) and growing at
a rate of 3.5 percent annually.

In considering Party politics in the rural area, it is necessary to separate
two aspects: land tenure, that is, ownership or control of land, and agricultural productivity and efforts to increase it.

During the Viet Minh War years the overriding interest was high production, meeting food needs. There was little centralized planning, a
good deal of agrarian trial and error. Party policy, under Truong Chinh,
was to secure grain, not to frighten landowners with collectivization—a
theme, incidentally, that was used heavily by Franco-Vietnamese anti–
Viet Minh propaganda. The Party sought to rectify only the worst
excesses of landlordism and usury. As Lenin before him, Ho Chi Minh
used the land-to-the-tiller slogan to gain villager support. Confiscation
of land from the French and from rich Vietnamese for distribution to the
poor was part of the original 1930 ICP program and was reiterated
throughout the years except during periods of tactical silence. In 1945,
partly as a production incentive, the DRV abolished taxes in the region it
controlled, hoping it could derive sufficient operating income from
voluntary contributions and duties levied on goods moving through its
area. The program was a failure. Only later, beginning in 1950, did the

Party give systematic thought to plans and programs for the agrarian sector.

Party handling of land tenure divides into two phases, the economic leveling period, which began about 1950 and involved rent reduction and land redistribution, followed in 1958 by collectivization. It required first turning the rural society against itself through redistribution and then persuading the new owners to collectivize. This land-reform program—that is, redistribution, then collectivization—was not economic but sociopolitical in intent. It was a Maoist concept and had a threefold purpose: to destroy the existing rural social order, to secure Party administrative control over the means (and the fruits) of production, and, if possible, to increase food production. Clearly, beginning in 1950, the Party sought to ruin the wealthier villagers and such urban bourgeoisie as could be reached. Basic devices employed were punitive taxes and other economic measures just short of extortion.[6]

Redistribution of land in the North hardly made any sense in economic terms. The Red River Delta region under the French had the highest level of individual land ownership anywhere in Asia; 98 percent of the farmers in the delta owned the land they farmed. Further, some 60 percent of all land holdings in the North were less than one acre. Land reform was brought to villages where the difference between the largest and smallest holding in the village was less than a quarter of an acre. Recipients of the program, formerly the landless, were given on average a half hectare per family, while one hectare was considered the minimum acreage to support a family. But it was not the Party's intention to establish a viable, privately held land-tenure system, hence an unworkable land-reform program actually was in its interest.

By 1955 the first of the three objectives—smashing the old rural social order (treated in detail below) had been accomplished. There was, in addition, some economic leveling. Official statistics say 700,000 hectares of land—chiefly French-owned, government-owned, or owned by those who moved to the South—were distributed to 1.5 million landless. But, it was found, these changes in title led to a capitalist struggle among farmers. The difference between richer and poorer villager remained, the richer having draft animals and available credit, the latter having land but not the wherewithal to farm it. Thus, although the Party succeeded in shattering the rural social order, it did not break the rural economic order.

Food production obviously became of increasing concern to the regime after it assumed power. Truong Chinh led an ambitious and generally successful campaign to put some 300,000 fallow hectares back into production, restore the water conservation system, and increase grain yields. The stated plan in 1955 was to double rice production in five years. This goal was not reached. Harvests fell short of requirements, and the difference was made up through food grants from foreign sources. The gross increase in rice production during the five-year period—from 3.6 million to 4.1 million metric tons—would have been more impressive had there not been a corresponding 3.5 percent per annum population growth rate. Probably the goal of doubling rice production in five years was unobtainable, but the effort was harmed by a number of factors: mismanagement, Party cadres who went down to the villages in ignorance but with determination and ideological blindness, fear of the land-reform program, bad weather, and stubborn resistance by farmers who subtly sabotaged the effort. Still, all of this was apart from the essential problem of a poverty-ridden agricultural sector. Farming in the DRV was labor intensive, a hand-tool operation, the most expensive form of farming there is. The DRV had an antiquated agricultural plant inherited from the French, one with inadequate machinery, insufficient fertilizer and other chemical additives, and consequently, an extradorinarily low level of productivity.

The period of economic transformation (1958–60) essentially was an effort to get Party control over the means of production. In the rural sector this meant collectivization. As we shall see below, the program ran into serious peasant resistance.[7]

The collective system was installed by and for the Party. It, and not the state, is the central administrative authority at the basic level. The collective's administrative council (about 200 families) is headed by the local Party secretary. It reports upward through the Party apparat, not through the governmental structure, all the way to Hanoi. The reason for this is that the collective is not seen simply as an economic production unit, but as a basic sociopolitical unit.

Not until 1960 and the first five-year plan can it be said that agricultural production (as opposed to social change) became the major determinant in the Party's agricultural policy. By this time collectivization was well established as a social system, but not as a means of production. The 1960–65 five-year plan sought to rectify this and put agricultural productivity in command as a policy. The plan called for an annual food production goal of 9.5 million tons by 1965 and for deriving from the agricultural sector an economic surplus that could be transferred to heavy industry. The goal could not be met and, in turn, doomed to failure the plans for the surplus.

Transition to socialism also meant full development of DRV heavy industry; and, beginning in 1955, enormous, even disproportionate, emphasis was put on industrialization. A good case could be built against such a policy. After all, the DRV was a society in which the agricultural sector was nearly synonymous with the economy. There was no true heavy industry, not even much light industry, and from an economic standpoint it was questionable whether the country's meager resources should go into industry at the expense of agriculture. In the South, Diem made the deliberate decision to keep his country agrarian on the grounds that in a world growing ever more hungry, a country with a productive agricultural economy is in the best possible situation. But in the North, dogma dictated industrialization.[8]

Most of the first five years—1955–60—were devoted to economic restoration: getting the mines back into production, reopening the 150 or so larger-sized economic enterprises inherited from the French, renovating the transportation and communication systems, and restoring electrical production. These were tasks plagued by lack of technical skills; after Geneva, all 47 French engineers at the Nam Dinh textile plant, with its 12,000 workers, departed for home; the Hon Gay coal mine complex, with 11,000 miners, had only 2 Vietnamese technicians where once there were 150 French engineers.

The heavy industry effort, unlike agricultural collectivization, had a purer form of economic motivation. Changing the social order or counterrevolution hardly entered the picture. Industrial workers— whose numbers rose from 20,000 to 40,000 between 1957 and 1960— were treated as a privileged minority, receiving better food and social services than any other group, to compensate for being driven mercilessly. There was considerable aid from the outside. During the late 1950s, half of all DRV revenues came through bloc aid, in itself no small accomplishment.

Results in heavy industry, modest by Western standards, were considerable if compared to other developing nations. By 1960 the DRV had achieved a good start in industrialization, and its prospects were bright. All this was cancelled, however, by the decision to put the country's resources into war in the South.

In September 1960 the Third Party Congress met in Hanoi to receive the nation's first full five-year plan. It was an ambitious program, seeking to raise agricultural production by 50 percent, to increase industrial output (the norms varied by sector) an average of 14 percent, to nationalize the economy (i.e., get full Party control over the means of production), develop managerial capability, increase workers' technical skills levels, provide more consumer goods and public welfare programs, and build up the country's armed forces—all to be funded by Socialist allies. The program soon was in shambles. By 1963, when the plan was more or less officially scrapped, industrial output had risen only 6.5 percent; rice production that year was 13 percent below 1962's.

EXTERNAL RELATIONS

With its limited resources and its psychic need for external sustenance, the Party could not have won the Viet Minh War without outside support. Nor, probably, could it have maintained itself and then asserted full control over North Vietnam without additional aid. In the last crucial years of the Viet Minh War, large quantities of war matériel and logistical supplies poured in from the PRC and the USSR. But in the traumatic first postwar days, when disease and famine stalked the land and the chaos of war was replaced by mass exodus (6 out of every 100 persons), the battle against anarchy and disintegration had only the thinnest margin of outside support advantage.

Logistical difficulties during the war, followed by trouble during consolidation of power, impressed on the leadership the need for reliable sources of outside military aid. This was a conclusion driven home long before the ambitions of war in the South began to develop. The DRV had virtually no armament production capacity. It needed a dependable source of guns both for internal security and for possible external use later. That fact conditioned Party and state external relations from 1954 onward.

Beyond the aid required for survival—emergency food shipments and weapons—was the vast, nearly unlimited requirement for money to fund the industrialization and economic development programs then on the drafting board. Clearly, these could be funded only by outsiders. Thus, whatever the sentiments of the Party leaders regarding the world, they literally were driven by economic necessity into a close relationship with the only sources of essential supplies—the USSR, the PRC, and Eastern Europe. Official figures indicate that nearly 40 percent of the 1955 DRV budget was derived from foreign aid, although probably the actual amount is closer to two-thirds. This declined steadily over the next five years, to 20 percent at the start of the five-year plan.

The price of PRC and USSR support had been high at Geneva and continued so in the postwar years. In fact, the great trauma of foreign relations, in retrospect, was the Geneva Conference and the sacrifices the Party leaders came to believe they had made in subordinating their interests. The feeling continued to rankle, but the DRV had little choice. If it was to continue to receive vital aid it must continue to defer; for example, to sacrifice postwar French cooperation in the name of bloc solidarity.

At the time the DRV cast its lot with world communism in the early 1950s, the movement was seen as a historically invincible monolith. Shortly thereafter the monolith disintegrated, and the DRV found itself caught in the Sino-Soviet entanglement. For the DRV, the dispute both isolated it and allowed it greater latitude and freedom, the first because the disputants were willing to sacrifice relations with Vietnam in the name of the dispute and the latter because the dispute diminished the demands Peking and Moscow could levy on Hanoi. Over the years the Party sought to walk the line between the two contenders, playing one off against the other, although general Lao Dong sentiment was that the lack of Communist solidarity or proletarian unity would be blamed chiefly on the Chinese. In its never-ending stream of criticism of both parties on the subject, the Vietnamese Communist hierarchy boldly threw the most sacred tenets of the Marxist catechism into the faces of world Communist leaders over the years.

In mid-1956 the USSR, without consulting Hanoi, introduced in the United Nations the idea of two Vietnams, a move the DRV was obliged to denounce. The USSR subsequently reversed its position. Ho Chi Minh and Le Duan led a mission to Moscow in July 1957 that Party historians describe as a major event in modern Vietnamese history. Ho later said that the subject of unification was discussed and that there was complete agreement on the subject. Apparently Ho indicated long-range plans for stepping up armed struggle in the South and secured certain promises of assistance; probably Ho left the USSR leaders concluding that the Vietnamese secretly backed them in the Sino-Soviet dispute.

USSR aid during the Viet Minh War as well as in the immediate postwar years was less lavish than Chinese aid, on the order of one to two. In July 1955 a USSR-DRV $100 million aid agreement provided Burmese rice to meet the famine condition in the Hanoi region. In the next five years, the USSR supplied the DRV with forty-three industrial and light industrial plants along with the services of some 300 technicians, mostly in the mining and power-production sectors. USSR aid during the first five-year plan was concentrated in agriculture and telecommunications. By 1963 it was running about equal to that of the PRC, about $330 million per year. An additional $100 million per year came from Eastern Europe.

The PRC was the oldest and initially the most generous supplier of economic and military assistance to the DRV. Military aid during the Viet Minh War is estimated at $500 million; economic aid was at least $200 million, possibly more. Under the first postwar aid agreement, signed in December 1954, the Chinese helped rebuild the rail and road system, the postal-telephone-telegraph system, and the Hanoi waterworks. In the next five years, PRC technicians constructed twenty-eight sugar-processing plants, fourteen rice-polishing mills, and several consumer-goods factories. PRC aid during the period was running at twice the rate of the USSR's. There were 2,000 Chinese technicians on duty, nearly seven times as many as from the USSR. During the five-year plan the PRC aided in the development or expansion of the chemical, electric power, and metallurgy industries.

Party leaders initially were impressed by the economic changes being wrought by the Chinese Communists and sought to emulate them. But many programs failed to yield the expected results, and disillusionment set in (as happened in China); something of a doctrinal dispute broke out among leaders and cadres over which was the best model for development of Vietnam—Chinese or Soviet.

Lao Dong Party relations with fraternal parties around the world in the 1950s generally can be described as nominal and correct. The Party in Vietnam was preoccupied, first with the war against the French and then in establishing itself in power. There was not a great deal outsiders could do, beyond providing no-strings aid, nor a great deal the Party wanted them to do. International intraparty developments had little effect on the Lao Dong Party. The de-Stalinization program, for example, had none of the impact that it had on the parties of Eastern Europe.

SOCIAL TRANSFORMATION

The Party's self-appointed duty to move the Vietnamese society to socialism/communism, as noted earlier, had a noneconomic dimension. It involved societal discipline, what officially was termed completing the democratic reform. This meant overturning the old social order and replacing it with a new one, peopling it with the new Vietnamese man, thinking new thoughts. It was a cultural revolution in the same sense in which that much-misunderstood term was used in China. Essentially an organizational activity, it also had a darker side of internal security—the struggle against the counterrevolutionaries. In the end it was a success, for it created a well-disciplined, submissive society, ruled by the all-intrusive Party properly guided by communism—in fact, the very model of a Marxist-Leninist society.

This was no mere act of surfacing the Party apparat or bringing Marxism-Lenism into the open, although there was that. Prior to 1954 most Vietnamese, even in the Viet Minh−controlled area, knew little about communism, and what they (especially Catholics and sect memers) did know, they rejected. Never were the Vietnamese given any sort of a clear choice between communism and noncommunism. The Party always had muted its dogma in public output and obfuscated its role within the Viet Minh. It was this ignorance the Party now set out to change by propagation of ideology, that is, explaining and selling various notions about the nature of society, and, more importantly, by integrating the Party into the everyday life of the average Vietnamese.

It was a labor of many parts, and required:

* Creating class consciousness among ordinary Vietnamese, raising their revolutionary consciousness within a class framework

* Perfecting special institutions, such as the agitprop apparat and the emulation movement, to mobilize and motivate the people

* Raising the quality of socialist life, as it was termed—that is, providing socialist solutions to existing social problems

* Launching a vast new security program to eliminate counterrevolutionaries and to eradicate undesirable thoughts and negative behavior

* Above all, ensuring that the Party and its ideology monopolized the
  nation's thought process or as the Third Congress resolution expressed it, "Marxism-Leninism must absolutely dominate the moral
  life of the country, become the ideology of all the people, be the basis
  on which is built a new morality. This is the socialist revolution in
  the ideological field.[9]

    The entrenched villager in the rural area, as might be expected, was
the main initial target of the Party's struggle for social reformation.
Eventually this became three specific village targets: the traditional-
minded villager, the land-owning farmer, and the Catholic.
    The struggle began in 1951 when the Party launched its Land Reform
campaign, which, as mentioned earlier, had to do less with either land or
reform than with a sociopolitical attack on the existing rural social order.
Expropriation and confiscatory taxes were less important in purpose or
result than the facts of arrest, denunciation, kangaroo court trial and
summary execution, and the general terror that the campaign evoked.
The attack was led by Truong Chinh, walking in the path of Maoism and
aided by a corps of imported Chinese Communist advisors. The intent
was not to terrorize the villagers but to organize them along certain lines.
The terror developed because of villager resistance and misdirected
Party energies, and because Party cadres at the basic level misused
authority.
    Into the 15,000 villages of North Vietnam in the summer of 1955
went legions of young Party cadres, armed with ideological zeal and
determined to build the brave new world. In the name of land reform
they set about to destroy a village social structure that had existed for a
thousand years. Village life—a temper that had been placid with at least
the normal harmony found among peoples who live together intimately
for generations in relative equality—suddenly was transformed into a
jungle of animal rage. Overnight the village became pathological.
    The cadres did not come in the name of economic equality; in fact,
economics hardly concerned them at all. Nor were they there to see that
justice finally triumphed against the local villains, for they worked
without dossiers of evidence and indeed saw nothing *personal* in what
they were doing. They were engaged in an abstract act: they had come
to eliminate, not people, but a social order.

First the village administration was reordered, the poorest (or least successful, or most alienated) inhabitants put in charge as the local Land Reform Committee. Then, under the authority of the Population Classification Decree of March 2, 1953, which quite candidly declared as its purpose to "separate our friends from our enemies," all villagers were classified into one of five categories.[10]

Next were established People's Agricultural Reform Tribunals (Toa An Nhan Dan Dac Cai Cach Ruong Dat Biet), which denounced, tried, and jailed or executed certain villagers. Tribunals apparently operated on a quota basis.[11] If insufficient exploiters were available, having never existed (some villages had no rich) or having fled, the quota fixed by Hanoi was met by expanded definition. The crude test of exploiter-exploited was land holdings or wealth—the difference being a few acres of land, or income of a few hundred a year—although this was only a guide. It was not uncommon for an individual owning no land to find himself listed as an exploiter, and even someone classified as a landless peasant sometimes owned land but had low social status in the village.

Against these few hapless village exploiters was turned the wrath of the other villagers, created by what was called mass mobilization. The villager everyone had known all his life went before the tribunal (acting as a court, but outside the DRV legal system, with no codified or procedural instruction) to hear his verdict handed down: death or imprisonment. Party cadres deliberately created a condition of social pathology by working on the emotions of individual villagers, the hatred born of past frustrations, the avarice of poverty, the long desire for a neighbor's field, and the remembered (or imagined) past grievance now demanding retribution. Thus, the process brutalized all. In degrading the prisoner, the accuser also was condemned.

The price paid was high, although how high in lives probably will never be known. Estimates range from 50,000 to 100,000 dead. In retrospect, it is not the numbers that chill and sadden so much as it is discovery of the Party motive that was the driving force behind this great social experiment. The cadres did not act in passion, in the heat of revolutionary determination to correct ancient wrongs, which would help explain, even if not justify, the bloodletting. Rather it was, in the name of Party ambition, the exploitation of basically decent people by manipulating their emotions so as to surface the dark stain of inhumanity that exists in all of us. This dehumanized the Land Reform campaign far beyond mere murder, and it created within the society a subliminal force of which it still has not rid itself.

Initial Party reaction to the resistance that developed was to intensify counterrevolutionary measures. Additional troops were deployed to the countryside to back up the cadres. This failed, and the tide of open opposition surged to dangerous new levels by mid-1956. Apparently differences in viewpoint developed between Party cadre and PAVN officer, possibly because the military officers were less ideologically oriented. PAVN officers reported to Hanoi rising tensions in the rural areas and the possibility of serious trouble.

Then, a second phenomenon developed. The excesses turned inward on the Party. As often is the case, in fiction and in life, the monster created in the laboratory turns on its creator. An obscure but deadly internecine struggle in the guise of land-reform efforts broke out among Party members at the basic level. Some used the program for personal revenge, others to defend certain villagers by denouncing the denouncer. Many good Party members and cadres were swept up in the net of accusation and were tried and jailed. Land reform became a neutral club that any clever Party member could use to his own advantage.

Nothing could possibly alarm the leadership in Hanoi more than the prospect of Party self-destruction at the basic level. The leadership moved quickly. The denunciations began. Ho Chi Minh publicly apologized in August 1956 for "the errors committed while unifying the peasants," as he carefully expressed it, and promised to correct damage done by Land Reform Committees. The Party Central Committee met in September, apparently more concerned with intra-Party conflict than with excesses against villagers. Debate on the subject turned into something of a doctrinal standoff, for nothing conclusive came out of the session.

But decisive action soon followed. At the Party's Tenth Plenum (October 27–29, 1956), land reform became an anathema overnight. General Giap was chosen to perform the official act of contrition, during which he cited error in great detail.[12]

Truong Chinh was fired, as were Land Reform Committee members Ho Viet Thang and Le Van Luong; other heads rolled, figuratively.[13] Prison doors opened to some 12,000 alleged exploiters. Ho signed a decree abolishing the hated tribunals. There was an orgy of Party breast-beating, along with some lurid newspaper accounts of life in DRV prisons. It all quickly became systematized into a Rectification of Errors campaign.

But the momentum had become too great. Social carnage in the village had moved beyond mere resistance. Conciliatory gestures were too late; the situation had to get worse before it could get better.

Open rebellion broke out in November 1956, the month that would be recorded as the nadir in the Party's postwar fortunes. The product of villager and Catholic rage and fear, rebellion began, most humiliatingly, in Ho Chi Minh's home province of Nghe An. In two weeks the rioting and insurrection had spread throughout most of the province. A full PAVN division took nearly a month to put down the uprising. Elsewhere in the country other uprisings developed. The worst of these was near Vinh, beginning on November 8 with a confrontation between demonstrators and Party cadres over Catholic attempts to petition the International Control Commission in Vinh for assistance in moving to the South, claiming they had been prevented from doing so earlier. The Party moved in special agitprop teams, backed by military units, to dissuade the petitioners. A riot ensued, and disorder spread throughout the province. Rioters burned government and Party offices and vehicles, seized arms from local militia (many of whom defected to the rebels), and began a march on Vinh. Three days of heavy fighting followed, between some 10,000 militant Catholics and some 20,000 PAVN troops. The toll in this rebellion never could be established by outsiders. Testimony of eyewitnesses who later fled to the South indicated that at least hundreds were killed. Bernard Fall claimed that 2,000 were executed and 4,000 jailed or expelled to the South, but this could never be verified.[14]

Resistance by the Catholics, in many ways, was considered more serious than villager reaction to excesses of the Land Reform campaign. The Party always had been officially antireligious, holding that no Party member could believe in an anthropomorphic being and still be consistent with the scientific principles of Marxism-Leninism, but there never had been the hostility of, say, the Bolsheviks toward religion in Russia. Further, the great bulk of potential Catholic troublemakers had left the country in Operation Exodus, hence the Catholic rebellion was unexpected. The Party quickly made conciliatory gestures. Freedom of religion was officially reproclaimed a state policy. Ho Chi Minh received a group of churchmen and apologized. Indemnification was paid for destruction in cathedrals and seminaries.

Still another element of society—the intellectuals—developed as a source of dissidence in late 1956 and early 1957. Emulating the wisdom of Mao Tse-tung and his Hundred Flowers campaign in China, the Party invited intellectual critics, grown restive since Geneva, to comment on the social scene. The offer was accepted, and out of the November 1956 Vietnam Congress of the Vietnam Democratic Party (a kept party of intellectuals in the Fatherland Front) came stinging denunciations of the lack of political freedom in the DRV and the effects of the anticapitalist programs on the cost of living. As in China, the torrent of criticism, satiric fiction, and barbed poetry soon reach flood stage, much of it appearing in the Democratic Party's magazine, *Nhan van* (Humanism). The Party suffered this verbal assault silently for a few months, then, again as in China, abruptly canceled the invitation to free criticism. *Nhan van* was suppressed and Party cadres instructed to track down and destroy all back issues. Some of the intellectuals were jailed. The Nhan Van affair, as it came to be called, was the Party's first and last experiment with freedom of expression.

Eventually the resistance was broken and dissent quelled. The Party bided its time, then returned to original purposes. Land reform was resumed under a new name in 1959 and was pushed through to completion, this time with no serious difficulty. After a hiatus, an organizational campaign began against religion. Priests were denounced, accused of engaging in antigovernment activity, and generally villified as a source of various social ills, particularly in the rural areas. Tight organizational controls were clamped on the Catholic Church, and non-Vietnamese clergy were expelled, reducing the hierarchy from 5 bishops and 300 priests. Parochial schools were closed when the church refused to transfer authority for teacher appointment to the state. All activity by church officials was carefully proscribed, and there was a general effort to discourage church attendance by all but the elderly.

As General Giap noted in his Rectification of Errors speech, considerable resistance to the regime had been offered by Montagnards, the ethnic minorities constituting 15 percent of the population in the highlands. Except for terse references in Party documents, virtually nothing is known of this resistance—whether it was widespread, whether it involved bloodshed, how many tribesmen it involved. In the postwar years the Party pushed its control and its agricultural system into the highlands determinedly, but it appeared at the same time to attend to Montagnard sensitivities regarding language, local customs, and social order. Some Montagnards were able to rise in the Party system, but the price was substitution of Party for tribe.

Gradually the Party established complete control of the society. It succeeded because it put together the proper combination of means and methods. It developed an extraordinarily effective communication system to motivate the general population. It imposed an overlapping system of social organization to enmesh the individual. It installed a formal internal security apparatus involving population controls (documentation, travel permits, identification papers) along with an effective network of informers and compulsory surveillance by mass organizations operating through a block warden system. Collectively these institutions gave the Party iron-grip control. It made a repetition of the 1956 rebellion, or any other sort of revolution, practically impossible.

The turmoil of the first postwar years had been traumatic, but the Party's moral certitude was unshaken. No reason was seen to revise the standing principle that it is better to kill ten innocents than to permit one enemy to escape.

Developments in North Vietnam in 1956 were important. The defeat suffered by the Party was a major one, but little of what happened that year was reported abroad and so never entered the world's consciousness. Events in Vietnam were overshadowed. The Hungarian uprising and the Suez crisis claimed the front pages of newspapers in the West. Once again, the Party in Vietnam was the beneficiary of some undeserved good luck.

ASSESSMENT OF THE FIRST YEARS

By the end of 1960, although it was a bad year on the farms because of poor weather, the DRV internal scene had markedly improved. Looking back, it was clear that the low point of the Party's first half decade in power was 1957; cadres later privately referred to "the crisis year of 1957." That was the year the land-reform program triggered uprisings; the year the South did not collapse and, concurrently, the Party's political struggle strategy proved a failure, but with the Party in no position to effect a major shift of policy; the year relations with the USSR went into great disarray (the proposal of two Vietnams in the U.N. and its subsequent denunciation by the Party). But by 1960 a general sense of optimism and confidence had returned. The land collectivization program was moving ahead. A new trade deal with the USSR promised to increase imports by 50 percent and, in addition, the USSR had reversed itself on the U.N. membership issue. A new aid agreement had been signed with the PRC. Industrialization efforts, although falling short of quotas, were impressive; total industrial output had increased 20 percent per year in the last three years of the decade. Counter-revolutionaries had been gotten in hand. Ngo Dinh Diem's troubles in the South were on the rise. Particularly in comparison with the South, the DRV's prospects appeared highly favorable as the new decade began. At the onset of its adventure in the South, this was the fundamental DRV condition:

* It was bigger, richer, and more populous than the South.

* It had internal order and strong social and governmental institutions, unlike the sociopolitical vacuum, the condition of near anarchy, in the South. The DRV, as a government, was well organized, run by a corps of Party cadre whose administrative skills had been honed by a challenging war and whose experience was a continuing one, reaching back nearly two decades. The repressiveness of the immediate post-war years, epitomized by the crushing of the Nghe An uprising in 1956, had given way to a generally more moderate and tolerant attitude toward the rural population.

* There was far less social pathology compared to the South, which was cursed by divisiveness. An accommodation had been made with the ethnic and other minority groups.

* It was secure. It had twenty first-rate infantry divisions composed of the cream of the battle-hardened fighting men of the Viet Minh War.

* Economic prospects were good. Industrialization was well underway. Revenues, still in generous amounts, were coming from abroad in the form of bloc-nation economic assistance programs. The economic development program, modeled after that of Communist China, appeared to be succeeding, and economic observers at the time placed the DRV's industrialization effort only three to five years behind China's.

In short, the DRV had much going for it. Despite this, or perhaps because of it, plans now were being made to liberate the South by military force.

Chapter 7

Unification

The goal of unification, one Vietnam under the Party's banner, became an objective as soon as it became a problem at the 1954 Geneva Conference. Not liberation of the South, nor a revolution in the society there, but unification alone was the Party's undeviating purpose until it was achieved nearly twenty years later. The Party never hid this fact, as even a casual inspection of its pronouncements and leaders' speeches through the years clearly demonstrates.

In considering the Vietnamese idea of unification, it is necessary to distinguish between ethnic identification and national unity. The Party's drive for unification was not in the modern political meaning of, say, Italy or Germany in the nineteenth century or, in another sense, the American Civil War, but was a premodern expression of ethnic identity.

At some point, or perhaps from the very start, unification passed from mere Party policy to holy crusade, from goal to obsession. Consider this typical passionate assertion from Ho Chi Minh: "Each day the Fatherland remains disunited, each day you (of the South) suffer, food is without taste, sleep brings no rest. I solemnly promise you, through your determination, the determination of all our people, the Southern land will return to the bosom of the Fatherland."[1]

The question of how exactly to deal with the South had long plagued the Party. Failure to assign priority to the region in the early 1950s resulted in the Party's inability to seize the opportunity offered by French withdrawal. Later in the decade, uncertainty as to how to

proceed continued, although the picture painted by some historians—
the Party passively waiting for the South to collapse—is inaccurate. The
Party had a clear objective, unification, and a strategy that was dynamic
even if unsuccessful.

The Party's Sixth Plenum (July 1954) restated the situation: Vietnam
was one and must be united. The revolution was proceeding in two
stages: building socialism in the North, liberation in the South. All
Vietnamese, the plenum declared, were duty-bound to aid the cause in
the South, although the South should be as self-contained and self-
supporting as possible so as not to drain away vital northern resources.
The plenum underscored the importance of monopoly Party leadership
to prevent rise of a breakaway bourgeois revolutionary force.

Strategy to achieve unification varied during the next ten years, but
the fundamental concept remained constant. While perhaps familiar to
many readers, this strategy is worth reviewing briefly.[2] Many terms are
used to describe it; *revolutionary war* is the one employed here. Its essence
is *dau tranh* ("struggle") of two types. The first is *dau tranh vu trang*
("armed struggle"), and it involves various military actions by main-force
and guerrilla units.[3] It primarily means practice of three-stage guerrilla
war, but also violence normally not associated with regular armed forces,
such as kidnapping and assassination. The second element is *dau tranh
chinh tri* ("political struggle"). It is composed of the three *van* programs:
dan van ("action among the people"), *dich van* ("action among the
enemy"), and *binh van* ("action among the military"). Collectively these
three *van* programs plus the violence programs of armed *dau tranh* constituted the revolutionary war. Every act, every statement by every
Communist Vietnamese, every decision from Central Committee
to village came within the scope and framework of *van—dau tranh*. The
doctrinal cement that held all this together is called *khoi nghia* ("general
uprising").

Of the many variations of armed *dau tranh*, or communist-style
warfare, two are of major concern to us. The first is what PAVN
Commander in Chief General Vo Nguyen Giap calls regular-force
strategy or big-unit warfare, which in turn can be of many types but
chiefly consists of the "independent fighting method" (the 1968 Tet
offensive, for example) or the "coordinated fighting method" (the
1965—66 campaign or the Easter 1972 high-technology-warfare campaign).[4] The second variation is protracted conflict, the so-called fifty-

year-war thesis. It pays major attention to and maximizes the contribution of political *dau tranh*, while regular-force strategy puts more premium on armed *dau tranh*. Twice over the years, each of these two doctrines dominated strategic considerations.

The two forms of *dau tranh* are seen as hammer and anvil or as the two prongs of a pincer. It is not possible, under revolutionary war theory, to be victorious using only armed *dau tranh* or only political *dau tranh*. Victory comes in properly combining them. Herein lay the source of great doctrinal dispute. How much of the resources, particularly manpower, should go to the armed *dau tranh* pincer, how much to the political? Which is the anvil, which the hammer? The disputants took positions along a continuum, armed struggle at one end and political struggle at the other: how far up or down the scale was proper?

Much Party policy making and activity for two decades can be fitted into the framework of the doctrinal search. In fact, the history of Vietnam from 1954 to 1975 is encompassed in the long sweep of the doctrinal stages designed to yield unification. There were four of these, admittedly an arbitrary division but necessary here for the sake of brevity.

THE COURSE OF THE WAR

The first of these four periods in the search for unification ran from the 1954 Geneva Conference to the Party's Fifteenth Plenum in late 1959. Unification was sought, in effect, by means of French diplomacy abroad and political struggle in the South. The sense of the 1954 Sixth Plenum contained the hope, as opposed to the expectation, that the French and other participants in the conference would "implement" the agreement and bring about unification. Meantime, political struggle pressure would be applied in the South to help topple the shaky Ngo Dinh Diem government. Whether the French could unify Vietnam (or wanted to) is questionable, but in any event it did not happen.

The second period was the revolutionary guerrilla war phase, from 1959 until late 1964, when unification was sought by means of a mix of armed struggle, in the form of revolutionary guerrilla war, and political struggle, through the instrument of the National Liberation Front. The expectation was that the two prongs could create sufficient social pathology, anarchy, and simple chaos to bring down the Diem government and lead eventually to a government amenable to unification. The strategy did indeed tear up the South Vietnamese society. It also was militarily effective. By 1964 the Party controlled two-thirds of the country's 2,500 villages. The balance of armed-political struggle shifted to the military end of the continuum. The People's Liberation Armed Force (PLAF) began to strike Army of the Republic of Vietnam (ARVN) units directly, seeking to eliminate ARVN reserve battalions one by one. By February 1965, few were left. Once an army's reserve battalions are gone—and it must still defend its fixed installations—it is at the mercy of the enemy, for the enemy can mass its forces and reduce one fixed installation after another. Defeat comes piecemeal.

February 1965 thus became the moment of decision for the United States—either to do nothing and see Communist victory, perhaps within weeks, or to begin full-scale combat with troops and air power to stop the Communist drive. When the latter fateful choice was made, it became a new war and brought the Party face to face with a new enemy.

The third phase employed the regular-force strategy and is informally called the big-unit phase. Unification would be achieved by slugging it out, the PLAF and PAVN (with the PAVN reluctantly assuming an ever-greater burden of combat) versus the ARVN, increasingly aided by the United States and other allied forces. Warfare became more conventional. It was a time of weapons conversion as both sides faced the fact that technology, within a decade, had virtually revolutionized the conduct of war. PAVN generals took over, stripping the PLAF of its best men for PAVN replacements.

This change of strategy was not a reaction to U.S. entry; rather, it predated it.[5] The switch from revolutionary guerrilla war to regular-force strategy war was a manifestation of the Politburo doctrinal dispute between, on the one side, General Giap, Le Duan, and the big-unit war advocates and, on the other, Truong Chinh and his protracted-conflict exponents. Despite PLAF success, Politburo doubts had grown as to whether revolutionary guerrilla war ever could actually deliver victory. That it could create massive social pathology there was no argument, but social disintegration of the South was not necessarily the same thing as unification. Hence the belief grew that more orthodox forces were required to deliver the final blow. Further, there was growing Politburo suspicion about the reliability of the apparatus in the South. The

Politburo felt uncomfortable with a system granting so much autonomy to unreliable southerners. When the end came—and it was seen as coming soon—the Party meant to have on the scene a completely loyal military force to ensure that the war was not won, and the peace lost, through some last-minute settlement that would (as in 1954) betray the cause of unification.

The tempo of warfare rose steadily, then climaxed with the 1968 Tet offensive, which extracted such a toll from PLAF units that it became physically impossible any longer to pursue regular-force strategy. But the campaign had produced an impressive victory in the name of political struggle: it had brought down the president of the United States by way of Lyndon Johnson's decision not to seek reelection. General Giap and Le Duan, who had masterminded the campaign out of faith in armed struggle, experienced bitter defeat while ironically proving what their doctrinal opponents had insisted all along, that victory could only be won through proper use of political struggle tactics. The latter continued to be vindicated, for the fact is that the American army never lost a single important battle during its eight years in Vietnam. The nature of the war was such, however, that winning battles did not deliver victory; it only blunted the armed struggle prong.

The fourth and final period, the talk-fight period, ran from 1968 to the end of the war in the spring of 1975. It was a complex mix of armed and political struggle and involved these actions:

* Renewed military activity in the South on a selective basis. Protracted conflict, after several years of disuse, again was expounded to cadres: victory would come if the enemy could be outlasted, outwaited, outendured. The southern buildup would continue.[6]

* Seeking of external support and aid from socialist and other nations and encouraging antiwar movements in the United States and around the world.

* Staging military offensives in Vietnam geared to U.S. politics. All three major campaigns of the war were in advance of U.S. presidential elections: the Tet offensive in the spring of 1968, the Easter offensive in the spring of 1972, and (as originally planned) the offensive of spring 1976.

* And, most importantly, maneuvering in Paris at the talks.

The Party (and DRV) attitude toward negotiations followed a straight unbroken line from the start of the war. Negotiation is a technique, not a method of conflict resolution; it is to be viewed solely on a tactical-strategic continuum.[7] It could be (and was) used to advance the cause, to disrupt the enemy's internal scene, to mislead enemy leaders, to divide the enemy camp. DRV/Party negotiators never regarded negotiation as a process of compromise, of give-and-take dealing. Nor was there ever any sense of obligation to an agreement once reached. The Paris Agreement—actually a cease fire arrangement, not a political settlement—bound the Vietnamese Communists to conditions that, if they had been fulfilled, would have destroyed the Party in the South and ruined all chance of unification.[8] But commitment to the agreement never was the intention, as candid postwar writings by top Party officials admit, much to the embarrassment of their foreign apoligists.[9]

Increased pressures—internal difficulties as well as the renewed and intensified U.S. bombing campaign—combined in late 1972 to force a change in Politburo doctrinal balance. This permitted DRV negotiators in Paris to separate military from political aspects in a settlement and to drop the requirement that the political future of South Vietnam be mapped out before a cease-fire was effected. Once that separation was made, the rest of the negotiations followed naturally. An agreement was announced on January 24, 1973. Essentially, it was a cease-fire arrangement that permitted withdrawal of U.S. military forces from Vietnam. Since the goal of unification had not been abandoned, it was clear from the start of the cease-fire that the North did not intend to leave South Vietnam alone. Supplies continued to flow to the South, along with personnel. The political struggle continued unabated. Preparations were made for another all-out military campaign sometime in 1976. Meantime, attention turned to improving the Party's internal condition.

THE PARTY IN THE SOUTH

The Party apparat in the South originally was an integral part first of the ICP and then of the Dang Lao Dong. It assumed a somewhat separate status after 1954 as the Southern Branch, and then in January 1962 the branch officially ws converted into the People's Revolutionary Party (Dang Nhan Dan Cach Mang), or PRP. After victory the PRP quietly died, officially so with the creation of the Vietnam Communist Party in December 1976.

A brief recapitulation of the Party's top leadership in the South is useful at this point. In the early years leadership was fragmented and amorphous because of the struggle with the Trotskyists and no single figure emerged. In the late 1930s Nguyen Van Tao developed into an important figure; present also were Duong Bach Mai, Nguyen Van Nguyen, Nguyen Van Kinh, and Nguyen Thi Minh Khai; all are important, but their exact status has never been established. Their casualty rate was high; only Tao and Kinh survived (the former, much later, to become a member of the National Assembly Reunification Committee and the later DRV ambassador to Moscow). Mai and Nguyen are believed to have been killed in the 1930s. For a period Miss Khai emerged as the leading official in the South, acting as Nam Bo Central Committee secretary general, but was arrested in 1940 and died in prison during World War II. Her place was taken by Nguyen Van Tran until the formation of the DRV, when he went North and became active in governmental economic and later foreign affairs. Le Duan and then Le Duc Tho were ranking officials in the South during the Viet Minh War. In the immediate postwar period there was no clearly first-ranked Party official in the South. In 1959 (possibly as early as 1957) Huynh Van Tam appeared as Nam Bo Central Committee secretary general until he was exiled abroad in a diplomatic assignment in 1961 and his place taken by Tran Nam Trung. If Tran Nam Trung is a position, not an individual (as some analysts believe), then the leadership may have been in the hands of Nguyen Van Linh (alias Nguyen Van Cuc, Muoi Cuc, Muoi Ut) or possibly Pham Van Dang (alias Nguyen Van Dang, Pham Xuan Thai, Hai Van). In any event, Tran Nam Trung was replaced by Linh (as Cuc) in 1964. Later, when Party affairs were upgraded, General Nguyen Chi Thanh was dispatched to the South to take control. When he was killed (or died) in 1967 he was replaced by Pham Hung, who remained the leading Party official in the South throughout the remainder of the war and into the postwar period.

In ICP days (up to 1950), the division in Vietnam was three-way— Tonkin, Annam, and Cochin China—not North-South. ICP Interzone Five, or Trung Bo, extended from Tonkin as far south as Ninh Thuan province; south of it was Interzone Six, Cochin China or Nam Bo, including all of the Mekong Delta. The central committee of each interzone reported directly to the Party Secretariat. When the Lao Dong Party was created in 1951, the two interzones remained but were placed under the newly created Southern Branch Central Committee, or the Truong Uong Cuc Mien Nam (Central Office for South Vietnam, sometimes translated as Central Bureau or Directorate), a six-man committee headed by Le Duan and including Le Duc Tho.

After the Viet Minh War the Central Office was abolished and the Southern Branch became a truncated interzone (essentially what once had been Interzone Six). This was the time of regroupment, when more than 80,000 Party members and others went North, with a consequent drop in Southern Branch Party membership.[10] Until the arrival of northerners in strength in 1965, the Southern Branch consisted of those few original members who remained (probably around 15,000), plus regroupees as they began to return after 1959[11] and selected northern cadres on administrative and training duties. The twenty-one-person Southern Branch Central Committee essentially was a liaison group performing such special administrative duties as were necessary because of problems due to geography and security.

After the Fifteenth Plenum (1959) and the Third Party Congress (1960), much changed in the South. Basic strategy to achieve unification was altered. A new united front, the National Liberation Front (NLF), was organized in December 1960. A new Central Office—and Central Committee structure—was created to assume overall authority of Party affairs in the South. In January 1962 the PRP was formed.

The PRP called itself the Marxist-Leninist Party of South Vietnam, the principal member of the National Liberation Front, the vanguard of the struggle against Diem, the soul of the NLF, the engine of the revolution. It claimed to be communist but dissembled on its connection with the Lao Dong, usually describing it as a fraternal relationship. In fact, it was a straightforward continuation of the Southern Branch. It used the same liaison net and channels of communication, employed the same chain of command.

In 1963 a new Party element was created in Hanoi called the Committee for Supervision of the South. Its duties included administration of PRP affairs. It was headed by Le Duc Tho and included Nguyen Van Vinh, chairman of the DRV National Assembly Reunification Committee.

Chairman of the PRP Central Committee was Vo Chi Cong.[12] Huynh

Van Tam was secretary general. Later Tam went to Algeria as the NLF representative, and his place was taken by Tran Nam Trung.[13] The Central Office at this time was being run by Nguyen Van Linh, who, as noted earlier, had acted as secretary of the Southern Branch prior to 1964. When the war enlarged and higher Party rank was required, Linh was superseded by a Politburo member, General Nguyen Chi Thanh, and Linh became his principal deputy. When Thanh died (or was killed in an air raid) in mid-1967, he was replaced by Pham Hung. Linh stayed on as one of Hung's three ranking deputies. The other two were General Tran Van Tra (alias Tu Chi) as the principal deputy for military affairs (and later representative on the Joint Military Commission established under the Paris Agreement and still later chief of the Military Management Committee that ran the postwar military occupation of South Vietnam), and Pham Van Dang, the principal political deputy acting as the liaison agent with the NLF and other mass organizations in the South. Linh, as the third principal deputy, handled Party affairs.

The relationship of the PRP hierarchy to the Central Office has never been fully established by analysts, although it was clear that after 1965 many Party functions were assumed by the Central Office. It is possible that the chairmanship of the PRP passed from Vo Chi Cong to Tran Nam Trung even as the position diminished in importance. It also appears that Huynh Tan Phat may have headed the PRP or even been the ranking Party official in the South for a brief period, between the tenures of Tran Nam Trung and Nguyen Chi Thanh.

Important Party figures in the South during the war years included:

* Pham Hung, the Politburo figure so long missing from the Hanoi scene. He was Party secretary in the South in the later years of the war; he also served as PLAF political commissar.

* Nguyen Van Linh (various aliases), the Party's chief official in the South in the initial years of the war. Born in the South (1913) of northern parents, Linh was raised in the Mekong Delta. He began his revolutionary career in the mid-1930s; supposedly he was a protégé of Le Duan in the Viet Minh War period.

* Tran Nam Trung (whatever his true name), the early PRP secretary general and Provisional Revolutionary Government (PRG) defense

minister. Someone bearing this name emerged after victory and was treated publicly in a way indicating that he was a high-ranking Party figure.

* Vo Chi Cong (b. 1912, Quang Nam province), the durable old Anastas Mikoyan of the Party. He was the initial PRP Central Committee chairman and later the ranking Party official in the Zone Five (southern central South Vietnam) Party organization.

* Pham Van Dang (various aliases) (b. 1917, Vinh Long province), one of the early founders of the NLF; chief organizer for the Party and front organizations, including the all-important Workers Liberation Association.

* Nguyen Van Ho (b. 1917), a southerner who managed the Party's financial and fiscal affairs in the South during the war; postwar secretary of the Party organization in Ho Chi Minh City (as Saigon was renamed). He was apparently an important Party figure.

* Huynh Tan Phat (b. 1912, My Tho province), initially the chief Party theoretician in the South. He was Party chief for the Saigon—Gia Dinh Special Zone, secretary general of the NLF, president of the PRG, and later chairman of the postwar PRG Council of Ministers. As Party official, he has apparently faded somewhat in importance in recent years.

* Nguyen Huu Tho (b. 1910, Cholon), chairman of the NLF and later the PRG (and still later one of the two national vice presidents elected by the June 1976 National Assembly). Best known of the southerners, he was regarded more as a political front than as a person of authority.

* Three generals also emerged from obscurity after victory: Tran Van Tra (noted above); Le Can Chan, PLAF deputy chief of staff (for operations); and Dong Van Cong, PLAF deputy chief of staff (political commissar).

* Finally, Truong Cong Thuan, Pham Van Co, Hoang Son, and Tran Van Binh are other PRP figures about whom little is known.[14]

The apparat built in the South repeated northern experience and paralleled northern organization, the familiar troika.

The first was the social-based mass organization, a collection of various functional social movements, mainly the various liberation associations (farmers, women, youth, workers, students, and cultural), which greatly facilitated cadre efforts to mobilize the villagers and harness and control their energies. These social organizations were a fishnet dropped over the villager, totally enmeshing him. This resulted in a system that monitored all village activity, produced increased food yields, rooted out hostile villagers, and provided village militia and recruits for the PLAF. It also offered certain psychic satisfactions, such as a sense of participation in village decision making.

The second was the quasi-governmental apparatus. The administrative element was the revolutionary committee (or rev-com), collectively known as the revolutionary administration. It existed mainly at the village and district levels and was responsible for management of the liberation associations. It was the instrument with which the Party governed. Far above it was the Provisional Revolutionary Government, which was not a government, but a cabinet with a small staff. There was no governmental structure between the several dozen persons making up the PRG and the sprawling rev-coms of the liberated area. The two entities existed virtually independently of each other, with the Party contributing whatever liaison was necessary.

The third element was the Party structure, for most of the war called the People's Revolutionary Party. Organizationally, it was similar to the structure in the North. Geographically, the South was divided into three sections: Trung Bo Interzone Five, the northern part of South Vietnam; Nam Bo Interzone, the area to the south including the Mekong Delta; and the Saigon–Gia Dinh Special Zone.

PRP Chairman Vo Chi Cong and Secretary General Tran Nam Trung largely divided overall supervision between them in the early days, Cong being responsible for organization building, recruitment, the proselyting program, and agitprop and indoctrinational work, and Trung handling military affairs of the PLAF and liaison with the PAVN. Gradually, as the PAVN took on the burden of combat, Pham Hung and the Central Office apparatus assumed direction of military affairs. Throughout the war the PAVN chain of command was directly to Hanoi and did not go through the PRP system or even have much to do with it beyond nominal liaison.

The Party Central Office in the South was divided into the standard sections: organization, economic-financial, agitprop, front organization relations, intelligence-counterintelligence, communications, control, and so on. The echelon below the Central Committee was the province central committee (*tinh bo*) or city central committee (*thanh bo*), managed by a three-man secretariat (chairman, secretary, assistant secretary) interested chiefly in assuring coherent activity below it. The district level—the district central committee (*quan*) or town or portion of a city (*khu pho*)—was the main Party operating element in the South and, until 1964, the lowest operating level. It was responsible for all Party activity in its area and had considerable latitude in its operations. After 1964, the apparatus was extended to the village (*xa*) or street zone (*khu pho*), and this became the first echelon of Party work at the agency level, that is, in villages, schools, rubber plantations, factories, and the like. Under it were three to a dozen branches, *chi bo*, although day-to-day leadership usually was in the hands of a single full-time Party leader. The basic Party unit, the *chi bo*, was composed of one to seven three-man cells. It was the Party's "link with the masses."

A Vietnamese seeking membership in the PRP had to be sponsored by two Party members. Unlike the Party in the North, a potential member could be nonproletarian; bylaws stipulated that he be a "worker, middle-class peasant, *petite bourgeoise*, student, intellectual, Montagnard, or [an ARVN] deserter." Actually, the chief requirement was that the individual actively support the cause and possess a good record in this respect. His sponsors were responsible for both his indoctrination and his behavior during the probationary period, which lasted from four to six months depending on his social class.

The task of the Party in the South was threefold: to ensure the security of the cause, to help fund it, and to develop a broad and effective base of support for it. The first of these, what loosely could be called internal security, sought to eliminate all potentially hostile elements from the village. This was both a negative and positive effort—inducing support, where possible, through social organization; commanding it ruthlessly, if necessary, when persuasive methods failed.

The second activity—finance—was based on the assumption that the effort in the South should be as self-supporting as possible. Cadres came to the village, not in the spirit of what the Party would do for the villagers, but what the villagers could do for the revolution. Some of the effort involved squeezing from the village what was considered "economic surplus," but usually it centered on cadre efforts to increase agricultural production so that the cause would benefit without undue suffering by the villagers.

The third and major Party activity was in the domain between internal security and economic support. It was what the Party called "building uniform revolutionary thought and feeling among the masses." Out of the organization imposed on the village came mobilization. With the proper efforts by the Party, out of the mobilization would come motivation. Combined, this became the trinity: organization, mobilization, motivation. If there was a secret weapon in the Vietnam War, this was it.

WARTIME PARTY IN THE NORTH

The war years in the North were remarkably uneventful considering the enormity of the situation faced and the tremendous strain placed on the society. Party history from 1960 to 1975, in fact, is largely a record of events that did *not* happen. The war was not lost. There were no internal upheavals; no bloody struggle for power followed Ho Chi Minh's death; no Party purges were required. Neither participant in the Sino-Soviet dispute attempted to force a showdown in Hanoi. No Party congresses were held; even few plenary sessions of the Central Committee reported. This is not to say the war years were placid—it was a highly dynamic period—but there was a marked lack of that development scholars call the historical conjuncture, which makes up so much of written history.

The Party clearly was the leader in the war effort. To the Party goes credit for victory. It was able, in ten years of all-out struggle, to hone communism to perfection, both as creed and mechanism. The creed became national salvation, saving the country through proper application of Marxism-Leninism. The mechanism was the control of events, established by a compact leadership and maintained by a corps of experienced revolutionaries.

Credit for victory within the Party goes to the leadership, that is, to the Politburo and the operational code it developed. There are two elements to be kept in mind in judging the leadership. First, rule was, by design, a system of collective leadership. Second, each member of the Politburo drew his political power from a constituency within the society. Collective leadership was established at the time of Ho Chi Minh's death, in

September 1969. In practice it created the unwritten rule that while a decision that was highly objectionable to some member could be taken, no decision could be a total anathema to any Politburo member. Le Duan became the first among equals (or possibly even the eminent member), but he did not, nor could he, impose decisions that rode roughshod over the wishes of his colleagues. The arrangement was not exactly republican, but it did represent constituency power bases within the society. General Giap, for example, had the armed forces as his constituency, Le Duan the Party, Premier Pham Van Dong the bureaucracy, Tran Quoc Hoan the secret police, Truong Chinh the mass movements such as the Fatherland Front, and so on. Each ran his constituency, but it, at the same time, dictated the leader's actions; each constituency in effect became a political arena.

This arrangement worked where it did not work elsewhere—consider the failure of the troika experiment in Moscow in the same era—for several peculiar reasons. First was the influence of the "old boy" network. The men of the Poliburo had known and worked with each other for most of their lives, and all by now were past the half-century mark. There is enormous unity in such long associations, even those marked by ancient arguments and long-standing philosophical or operational differences of opinion; Confucians call it the unity of opposites. Second, there were no strong personalities among the eleven (originally thirteen) Politburo members. Ho Chi Minh was the only supreme egotist; some would say he had eliminated all the other strong egos over the years. Thus, there was not the usual precondition for a power struggle—two or three ambitious, strongly self-oriented contenders. Third, there was, in effect, the discouragement of the situation. The war pressed in, making any sort of power grab, which might trigger an internecine fight, extremely dangerous even if personally successful. Finally, no opportunity was created by the change of leadership. It is in time of political transition, when power moves from one individual to another or from one generation to the next, that the dangerous moment comes, particularly in a totalitarian society. In the case of the Lao Dong Party there was no transition. Save for the two claimed by death, the leadership of 1950 was also the leadership of 1975. Ho's death which could have precipitated such a dangerous moment, was cleverly handled by the Politburo eleven. They decided, unanimously, not to replace him, to go on exactly as before. Ho would remain, in spirit if not in body, the only personality.

As a cult, he proved more useful dead than alive. Such effort to forestall power grabs was tried many times elsewhere and failed, but it worked for the Dang Lao Dong.

At the Politburo level during the war, three major issues arose that can loosely be termed factional disputes, although it was more a case of agreeing to disagree.

The first was over proper strategy to achieve unification. This was discussed above: agreement that victory would come through combination of armed and political struggle, but what combination?

The second involved allocation of resources between the war in the South and nation building in the North; it largely concerned manpower. Actual decisions on allocation took on surge, or pendulum, characteristics. Heavy shipments down the Ho Chi Minh trail for several months would be followed by a period of relatively sparse supply, then by another intensive buildup. There was a low correlation to offensives in the South. Clearly, allocation of supplies was a manifestation of the collective leadership principle in action.

The third issue was over the proper handling of internal sociopolitical problems—war weariness, mismanagement of industrial production, self-aggrandizement by Party cadres, corruption, juvenile delinquency—summed up as the so-called problem of the quality of socialist life. Should the uplifting of society be attempted by emulation campaigns, moral exhortation, stimulating revolutionary ethics—that is, essentially Maoist means? Or should it be done by pragmatic appeals and incentives and by removing some of the strains on the society through lessened demands of war?

None of the three ever was satisfactorily solved during the war, but an agreement that all Politburo members could accept was maintained and the disputes thus kept within limits.

During the war years the Party continued to criticize the quality of Party members and cadres in what became something of an institutionalized harangue; the most frequent criticisms were for poor Party organization, poor internal Party discipline, and lack of revolutionary fighting spirit. While continual weeding out of hundreds, perhaps thousands, of members continued, there were no massive purges in the sense that term usually connotes, no ridding the Party of the treacherous or the disloyal by means of the usual firing squad. Figures on Party strength varied. In April 1965 the Party said it numbered 800,000 (4.4

percent of the population), while in April of the following year Ho Chi Minh told a visitor the figure was 760,000. By 1970, with a population estimated at 21.2 million, Party strength was estimated at 1 million; in 1975, with a population of nearly 25 million, at 1.2 million.

During the war years, as support demands increased and social problems multiplied, the Party moved deeper into the day-to-day state management of affairs. This was particularly true in the communes and in economic-fiscal management. To counter adverse effects of the war, Party controls in the economic and social sectors were increased through a series of Party directives issued in the mid-1960s. More and more activity in local government and in the armed forces passed to direct Party control. Security measures, the struggle against the ever-present counterrevolutionary, very nearly became a Party monopoly. National Assembly activity continued, including periodic elections. Candidates were nominated and campaigned through the Fatherland Front apparatus but were not, of course, competitive or partisan. Political activity was regarded as a means of mobilizing the population (and soaking up political energies), not as a means of expressing the public will. All in all, the system hung together remarkably—enduring the air strikes, suffering ghastly casualties in the South, managing through enormous economic deprivation—credit for which, again, goes largely to the Party.

FOREIGN RELATIONS

External relations during the war years were generally curtailed and involved or turned on the search for outside military and economic aid. This meant dealing almost entirely with the USSR, the PRC, and Eastern Europe.

The Party continued to walk the line carefully in the Sino-Soviet dispute. The earlier tilt toward Peking became more balanced as the war progressed. Attacks on the USSR, which had followed Khrushchev's ouster, stopped; there followed additional USSR military aid, including the vital surface-to-air missiles. If forced to choose in the dispute—as when the DRV sided with the USSR on the nuclear proliferation issue— a carefully designed balancing gesture followed within a few months.

The USSR made no serious commitments until about 1965. Premier Kosygin visited Hanoi in February 1965 and apparently concluded that the war was about won by the Communists. He promised rather lavish aid, both military and economic. Then victory receded, and the USSR, obliged to meet her commitments, found herself funding an apparently never-ending war with such expensive weaponry as SAM-2s, aircraft tracking systems, and MIG-21 fighter planes. The USSR attitude always appeared somewhat cool, probably because of Moscow's general view that local wars in Asia never seemed to serve her interests. But despite occasional nervousness, USSR aid during the war was extensive and at all times more than the minimum requirement.

The early PRC reaction to the war was the fear that the United States would use Vietnam as a springboard to attack China. It was important, therefore, that the United States not win. Beyond this, the war was viewed as an embarrassment to the USSR. Apparently the PRC was cool to the general idea of unification, preferring eventual emergence of two people's republics in Vietnam, but never was it willing to do those things needed to secure this arrangement. PRC military and economic aid was lavish, and some 40,000 People's Liberation Army troops served in Vietnam (antiaircraft gunners, railway and warehousing troops). Sino-Vietnamese relations during the 1960s generally were harmonious, although there were some bad moments: the summer of 1969, when for a few weeks it appeared a Sino-Soviet war might break out; the Cultural Revolution period, when the Chinese sharply criticized the Vietnamese conduct of war (especially the mid-1965 period, with publication of Lin Piao's *Long Live the People's War,* and again during the 1968 Tet offensive); at various times when USSR freight trains loaded with weapons and ammunition could not cross China because Peking had lost control in the provinces; and, finally, with the Chinese "ping pong diplomacy" gesture to the United States.

It is questionable whether relations with the two allies at any time could be termed close, but even if they were, that condition ended with what the Vietnamese considered the defection, first of the USSR and then the PRC, to the United States in the form of live-and-let-live policy variously termed peaceful coexistence, détente, ping-pong diplomacy, and so on. For the Party, dedicated to bedrock fundamentalism, this was unforgivable heresy. The Party's view was, and is, that the capitalist world must be destroyed and that this can be done only if a unified international proletariat conducts all-out revolutionary war. At one time in history this had been orthodox belief throughout the worldwide

communist movement, but times changed, and eventually it was embraced only by the Lao Dong Party and a few other ultraviolent communist elements in the Mideast and Africa. The Party tried and found
guilty both of its socialist allies, guilty of the sin of coexistence and, by
omission, international proletarianism.

This ideological desertion was augmented, in the Party's view, by a
more fundamental distaste for both Soviet and Chinese behavior, that
neither ally ever helped the Vietnam cause to the degree it deserved. Aid
was offered only after repeated appeals and then was insufficient and
granted grudgingly. Worst of all, it was given for the wrong reason—as a
ploy in the Sino-Soviet dispute, not because of genuine desire to help
achieve unification.

In the last years of the war, as the Chinese became increasingly
anxious (or appeared so) over USSR moves in Asia, it became plain that
Peking was not at all sure it wanted complete U.S. withdrawal from
mainland Asia, possibly did not want a clear-cut and decisive Vietnamese
Communist victory. The result was that Sino-Vietnamese relations
plunged to their lowest level ever. At the same time there was marked
improvement in Soviet-Vietnamese relations.

During the war years the Party and the DRV were active both in
Cambodia and Laos. Party cadres built the Khmer Rouge into a first-
rate fighting force, beginning in about 1970, and saw it win power five
years later. In Laos, for nearly a decade, the Party virtually ran the
Pathet Lao struggle against the rightists and neutralists and saw it, too,
take control of the country in 1975.

VICTORY

Suddenly and unexpectedly, in the first months of 1975, Vietnamese
communism's golden victory of unification was achieved. South Vietnam fell less to Party moral or military superiority than to simple chaos
and confusion. Grand strategy had called for 1976 to be the year of the
last hurrah. The military situation as 1975 dawned was judged to have
great ultimate promise but at the moment was a standoff. A localized
offensive in Phuoc Long province in January led to a greater victory
than anticipated—capture of the entire province. Two months later, a
second local victory yielded all of the highland province Ban Me Thuot.

Its capture turned out to be the final blow to organized South Vietnamese resistance. The unraveling began and never stopped until PAVN troops, atop Soviet-built tanks, crashed through the gates of Doc Lap Palace in the center of Saigon. The ARVN, which had fought so well earlier under far worse conditions, hardly fought at all. Chaos in decision making at the corps level, exacerbated by countermanding orders from Saigon, soon made it impossible for the ARVN to fight at all.

On April 30, the long war ended. The Party had achieved the chimera-like goal it had been pursuing with single-minded zeal since that initial gesture outside of the Versailles Conference hall in 1921. Vietnam was unified, under a Communist banner.

The cost was high. General Giap had admitted earlier to 600,000 casualties (at the time, 1968, the Pentagon estimate was 800,000), and it is safe to fix PAVN and PLAF total dead at one million. This was in a country whose population ranged, during the war, from sixteen million to twenty-five million. Nearly one out of every seventeen male North Vietnamese adults died in the war in the South. (A proportionate figure for the United States would have been fifteen million dead, the actual figure being about 49,000). Material loss in the North, through air strikes and bombings, probably was around $400 million (U.S.), again in a country with an annual GNP of about $1.7 billion. In addition, having put virtually all of its resources (and all it could garner abroad) into the war rather than into nation building, there was the vast economic loss of fifteen years of noninvestment. It left North Vietnam with the most stagnant, poverty-ridden, and backward economy of any country in Asia. The psychic loss—imposition of the most intrusive praetorian society anywhere on earth—is incalculable. These were only the costs to the North. In lives and material, the toll extracted from the South probably was double.

Doubtless the Party's wartime leaders felt the price paid was well worth the accomplishment of unification and will go to their graves never questioning the correctness of the course on which they set Vietnam three decades earlier. But history must judge it a Cadmean victory.

Chapter 8

The Party Today

Success in uniting Vietnam engendered, even required, a restructuring of Party organization and apparat. The victory presaged an end to the two-branch arrangement and a return to a single, all-Vietnam Dang Lao Dong. Thus, in forty-five years, the Communist movement in Indochina went nearly full circle, from a single entity dominated by the Vietnamese (the Indochinese Communist Party), to a nationally based organ (the Dang Lao Dong), to a geographic division of the Lao Dong Party (Northern Branch, Southern Branch), to conversion of the Southern Branch into a separate entity (People's Revolutionary Party), back to the Northern-Southern Branch structure, and finally back to the single nationwide Party[1] that makes special claims upon, although does not dominate, the two other Indochinese Communist movements in Cambodia and Laos. Conceivably, the wheel someday may turn to complete the circle, and an Indochinese Communist Party will emerge again.

The summer of 1976 witnessed unification of Vietnam in all institutions: Party, state, mass organizations. On July 2, 1976, the Socialist Republic of Vietnam (Cong Hoa Xa Hoi Chu Nghia Vietnam)[2] replaced the Democratic Republic of Vietnam (DRV), the Republic of Vietnam (GVN), and the Provisional Revolutionary Government (PRG). The National Liberation Front (NLF) merged into the Fatherland Front, the PLAF into the PAVN. All of the other social organizations, North and South, were similarly combined.

   As it set out on its new journey into the unknown future, the Party was marked by these characteristics:

* The society it had created continued to be asymmetrical, that is, a highly developed institution (the Party) erected on a relatively simple social base.

* The Party was ubiquitous, its cadres and members found everywhere, engaged and in command. No sector of the society could be denied to it, no activity was beyond its province. Officially it was omniscient, all-pervasive, totally intrusive.

* The Party was the omnipotent decision maker—by definition, infallible. With its superior wisdom as the rationale, the Party claimed for itself the role of supreme guide, mentor, and exemplar. It alone could determine the character society was to assume, regulate the direction and tempo of all social change, and, should error develop, assume authority to correct it.

* Because of these two characteristics, ubiquity and omnipotence, the Party exercised the right to monopolize social control. No legitimate power center could exist outside the Party. The right of revolution did not exist. Any challenge to Party authority was considered socially destructive, and the Party justified the measures it took to preserve the system it had created. In fact, all social rewards, as well as punishments, were to be dispensed exclusively by the Party.

   The great doctrinal question—in a sense unanswered—was what future role the Party was to play. Would it remain central to all? Would it remain relevant? Would it even remain necessary?

LAO DONG PARTY STRUCTURE

Organization of the Dang Lao Dong probably is more elaborate than that of any other political movement in Asia. In terms of sheer structure there never was anything in South Vietnam to equal it. The GVN and its attendant social movements were, by comparison, rudimentary and superficial.

Governing of Vietnam by the Communists is very much a matter of government by committee. In design, and to a large degree in reality, decision making at all levels is a collective act—group decisions with group responsibility. The Party committee, cadres are told, is the supreme leading organ. It represents the Party, is the nucleus of leadership and the symbol of solidarity. The committee leads and controls all activities beneath it, maintains close relations with parallel Party organizations, and answers to higher authority. It is the liaison between the Party and the masses outside the Party. It organizes the implementation of all Party policy. The Party committee represents the collective intelligence and strength of leadership of the entire system. Such is the official rationale for the Party committee.

The Party line—that is, party policy, sometimes called the mass line or general line—is fixed by Party resolutions, instructions, and orders from higher committees, the genesis being the Politburo if the matter is at all important. The Party line is binding on all, and every order issued subsequently is expected to be in harmony with it. As originally issued, the Party line is sufficiently vague in language to permit flexible interpretation at the intermediate (but not lower) level. Party line, of course, can change radically and suddenly, even reversing itself over-night. Committee decisions at all levels are based on the standard communist idea of collectivist agreement, called democratic centralism. This is defined in various Party documents of which this is typical:

> Decisions are made at committee meetings by majority vote and individual Party members must then obey. . . . The minority obeys the decision of the majority. The lower echelons obey the decisions of the upper echelons. All elements obey the Central Committee. . . . One shout and a thousand echoes. . . .[3]

This right of democratic centralism, as well as elections for congresses and central committees, can be suspended under Lao Dong Central Committee Resolution 135 NQTU (January 31, 1966), which allows each committee level to be appointed by the next higher committee.

Organizationally, there are three matrices of committees: central (or national), regional, and local.

The Central Committee level consists of an apparat of several hundred persons with the Politburo (eleven members plus two alternate members) at the pinnacle. The Central Committee, about eighty members plus alternates,[4] also includes a Secretariat (the Party secretary plus eight members), seventeen departments, and a separate Central Control Committee and Central Military Party Committee. In theory, the Central Committee operates under the ultimate authority in the system, the Party congress, of which there have been five or six since 1930.[5] Article 20 of the Party statutes calls for a Party congress of delegates every four years but permits postponement if "special circumstances" exist. Since the Party congress meets so infrequently, it never has developed the institutional strength experienced in other communist societies. The Central Committee is the chief governing body, but over the years it has tended to become a forum for high-level discussion rather than an actual decision-making organ. All important Party decisions, however, are issued in its name, usually as resolutions. The Central Committee meets several times a year in plenary or truncated session. But being a cumbersome body, it has tended to delegate much of its decision-making power to officers and standing committees, primarily of course, the Politburo.

The Politburo, by majority vote, does most of the actual decision making and writes the Party resolutions issued by the Central Committee. The nine-man Central Committee Secretariat formalizes these decisions and transmits them to the Party departments; it also handles important personnel assignments.

Beneath the Central Committee level is the intermediate committee level, or the Party's secondary apparat at the provincial, municipal, or autonomous (highland region, regiment in the PAVN) level. The intermediate committee consists of an executive central committee, a standing committee, a separate control committee, and a Party secretary. It is elected every two years by the regional Party congress. Usually consisting of ten to fifteen members plus alternates, and with a full-time staff, the intermediate committee is the main instrument by which Party policy is translated from directive to reality. It rewrites central directives to make them relevant locally. Implementation tasks in a Politburo directive, for example, might be quite different for a Party member on the Haiphong docks and for one in the mountains along the China border. In theory, the committee (as well as those above and below it) is elected, but during the Vietnam War democratic centralism was suspended. After 1973, Party congresses at the intermediate level again became more common.

Much of the intermediate committee member's time is spent at Party conferences, an institution that developed during the war years as something of a substitute for Party congresses. The conference brings together intermediate-level and national-level officials, both civilian and military, often mixed, although precisely who attends a Party conference depends on its specific purpose. Some, for example, a meeting of agit-prop cadres, may be narrow in purpose; others, for instance, a conference on a new system for allocating commune production, might have a broad objective. The conference helps keep officials from the center familiar with what is going on in the field, and it gives intermediate officials a chance to vent their feelings and air complaints to the central leadership. Most Party conferences deal with either domestic economic issues or internal Party affairs.

The tertiary, or basic, level exists at the district and below. Organizationally, its leadership resembles that of the secondary level (committee, secretary, control committee) except that the electing congress meets every year. Its chief concern is further localizing and implementing directives from higher headquarters.

The unit at the tertiary level is the *chi bo*, the Party chapter, or branch. It may be as small as three persons but usually is around fifty. It is organized within an installation or an enterprise—called an agency—such as a collective, factory, hospital, school, or PAVN battalion. It is managed by an executive committee elected or reelected every six months and is headed by a secretary whose work usually is in addition to whatever occupation he pursues (except in the military, where he is full-time as a political officer). The larger *chi bo* have a standing committee, a full-time secretary, and a separate control committee. The number of *chi bo* in Vietnam in the mid-1970s was estimated at 60,000, although the last published figure was in 1960, when there were 20,000.

The purpose of the *chi bo*, according to Party statutes, is "to link the Party with the masses, implement Party line and policy among the masses, and reflect the opinions, aspirations, and desires of the masses to the leading bodies of the Party." A special status for *chi bo*, established by a 1962 emulation movement, is the Four Good status, now held by about two-thirds of all *chi bo*. This status indicates superior achievements in (1) increasing production, (2) properly implementing Party policy, (3) making the *chi bo* relevant and central to local mass organization activity, and (4) strengthening Party organization and raising Party quality.

Under article 11 of the Party statutes, a separate Party structure exists for the armed forces. The basic level here is the Party chapter at the company level. There is not the formalized hierarchy upward in the military that there is in civilian Party ranks. There is a chain of command that parallels the military, reporting directly and finally to the Central Military Party Committee.

The *chi bo* is broken down into three-person *tieu to*, or cells. The *tieu to* is a psychic entity, the mystic unity of three, and has no administrative authority. In the agency there sometimes may be found, in addition to the Party chapter, one or more cells of elite Party members not part of the chapter; otherwise all members are part of the chapter.

The lower-echelon Party committee's major tasks are:

* Policy implementation: fixing guidelines, issuing orders, managing and supervising the unit's assigned tasks, and assuring that activity is in harmony with higher-echelon orders

* Local motivational work involving ideological indoctrination activity and assuring the dedication, spirit, and loyalty of all cadres and members

* Increasing unit performance—if a production enterprise, higher production; otherwise, greater efficiency and competency

* Party building: developing and strengthening local Party units in structural and institutional terms

* Cadre training, generally seeking to raise the quality of cadre performance

* Mass organization work: closely supervising local non-Party organizations such as religious groups and women's organizations

* Overseeing and attending to the material needs of the masses, that is, public welfare

The individual Party member, as part of the basic level, finds that being a member means enjoying the various rewards the society has to offer, social and psychic if not always material. In return, he is expected to (a) attend regular and special meetings faithfully; (b) study higher-echelon directives, major pronouncements, and officials' speeches (often aided with special briefings by a higher-level cadre) and also, to a lesser degree, familiarize himself with basic Marxism-Leninism and other ideological formulations; (c) act as an energizer within his agency among non-Party members in what is known as taking the leadership initiative, which means goading, haranguing, and prodding his fellow workers; and (d) engage in *kiem thao* sessions in which he criticizes himself or someone else—the Party method for harnessing social pressure in its own interests.

Party chapters are expected to get into everything: a chapter aboard a navy vessel conducts discussions on military leadership during long hours at sea; a chapter in Haiphong port considers ways of speeding up cargo handling; an antiaircraft battery chapter plans improved training techniques; a military hospital chapter urges doctors to improve their medical techniques; an ordnance plant chapter leads a crash production program; and on and on.

The Party chapter is not a trade union but a staff element. It does not work for the agency but for the Party. It is, in fact, the Party's chief instrument at the basic level. It must outline policies, dictate courses of action, monitor programs, uncover and rectify error. It provides what is called overall leadership, which means political, ideological, organizational leadership in both military and civilian sectors. The chapter can cancel local economic production plans; the chapter in the military can countermand a line officer's command. There are no limits to the leadership authority of the Party chapter, runs a common slogan—meaning no limits with respect to non-Party elements but, of course, within the confines of higher authority direction.

To become a Party member requires demonstration of zeal and determination, recommendation by two or more members, undergoing the scrutiny of Party inspectors, and successfully passing an oral examination that seeks to determine that the applicant has mastered basic Marxism-Leninism, is joining for no ulterior motive, and suffers no serious tendency to bourgeois thinking. Some cannot join: those from the middle and upper classes, comprador bourgeoisie classes, or, with some rare exceptions, Catholics. It appears that a quota system exists for women members—a ratio of five men for each woman being maintained—but this is officially denied. While somewhat difficult to join, it is easy to leave. Any member may quit the Party at any time, but he pays a certain social price for his action.

The seven duties of a Party member as paraphrased from various versions of the Seven Oaths that have been promulgated over the years, are:

1. Demonstrate constant loyalty to Party and cause.

2. Accept the Party line unhesitatingly, submerging all personal doubt or sense of opposition, and work tirelessly to implement it. Accept Party discipline, recognizing that a Party member's time and talent are not his to do with as he wishes but are at the absolute command of the Party, regardless of danger or hardship.

3. Take an active part in Party political work, that is, do not simply go along passively as a believer or well-wisher but engage in all Party activities: arrange and conduct meetings; sit on committees; participate in emulation drives, motivational campaigns, and agitprop programs; and instruct recruits.

4. Constantly raise one's personal ideological consciousness—becoming ideologically armed is the phrase—by mastering the principles of Marxism-Leninism and other Party doctrinal materials. Act as a transmission belt to the masses, explaining Party line and doctrine. Attend Party schools, newspaper-reading cell meetings, *kiem thao* sessions.

5. Set an example in productive labor; improve technical or professional competency.

6. Subject oneself to a regime of discipline, self-denial, and asceticism. Abstain from profiting from Party connections.

7. Maintain Party secrecy; be vigilant against counterrevolutionary activity, sabotage, threats to Party unity.

The basic, all-important rule is acceptance of Party authority, the instant unquestioning acquiescence of all lower-echelon organs, as well as all individual Party members, to decisions reached at higher levels.

While full-scale purges, Soviet style, are unknown in the Lao Dong Party, periodic purification is common. In fact, a constant process of weeding out the membership, called picking up the red card, is carried on by Control (the Politburo's Central Control Committee). This may be for suspected disloyalty, a failure to meet one's Party obligations, a lax attitude toward the value of Party membership, marked incompetence, or being involved in some major program failure.

Discipline short of expulsion includes public criticism, reprimand, and denial of participation in group activities for a specified period. If expelled, certain rights automatically are forfeited, such as access to higher education. Administration of disciplinary measures is by the control committee at the relevant intermediate or national level. This committee, of three to nine persons, is composed of central committee members and rank and file. The control committee at each level has three duties: to handle disciplinary cases and mete out punishment; to receive, appraise, and act on, if required, written complaints from members (often anonymous denunciations), and to audit Party fiscal records. All control committee actions must be approved by the central committee at the next higher echelon.

In June 1970 the Party introduced the Ho Chi Minh class, a special elite category of Party membership. It was aimed primarily at the PAVN and Party members within the military. It had three stated objectives: to raise the general quality of Party membership, to improve Party leadership, and to produce, through the mechanism of the Party in the armed forces, greater PAVN fighting efficiency. The program began with a new recruiting drive among the eighteen-to-thirty age group, with new and higher entrance requirements, and it also involved weeding out the worst or poorest Party members, perhaps as much as 10 percent of the membership.

The ratio of Party to population appears a matter of concern less than in, say, the USSR. There is, however, a determined effort to maintain the Party as a compact and integrated body distinctly set off from the masses and purposely kept small enough to permit exacting standards and enforcement of rigid discipline. But this is done primarily by careful recruitment and repeated indoctrination rather than by fixing limits on Party size.

Party membership growth, as extrapolated from official statements and statistics:

Period	Membership
First Party Congress (1935)	"a few hundred"
August Revolution (1945)	5,000
Second Party Congress (1951)	727,211 (or 760,000)
Third Party Congress (1960)	525,000
Fourth Party Congress (1976)	1,553,500

The Party's basic unit growth, as reported by Le Duc Tho at the Fourth Congress:

	1960	1976
Chapters (in North)	31,448	95,486
Basic-level units	16,340	34,545

If the Vietnam population (December 1976) was the figure indicated, just over 49.6 million, and Party membership 1.6 million, the Party represented 3.22 percent of the total population.

The postwar Party-state relationship remained essentially the same in the North while it was being extended throughout the South. The Military Management Committee—in effect a temporary military occupation by some nine infantry divisions—replaced the PRG and its network of local revolutionary committees, until it was superseded by full state unification in June 1976. At this time the North's state administration structure was imposed throughout the South. The southern military armed force, the PLAF, was incorporated into the PAVN. The NLF was merged into the Fatherland Front, as were all the NLF-associated social movements and organizations.

PARTY YOUTH

The Party founders were well aware that the ultimate success of their social experiment, in fact the very survival of the Party, depended on their work among the young. Special provisions were made from the start for organizing and indoctrinating the young.

Ho Chi Minh organized the first Party youth group in March, 1931 (the official anniversary is March 26) with some 1,500 charter members, according to Party history.[6] Over the years the organization has gone under various names: Indochina Communist Youth Group (1931–36), Democratic Youth Group (1936–39), Antiimperialist Youth Group (1940–41), National Salvation Youth Group (1942–56), Vietnam Lao Dong Youth Group (Doan Thanh Nien Lao Dong Vietnam, (1956–70), the Ho Chi Minh Lao Dong Youth Group (1970–76), and the Ho Chi Minh Communist Youth Group (since 1976).

The youth organization is patterned after the Soviet model of young-younger-youngest (Komsomol, Young Pioneers, and Little Octoberists) although with somewhat different age groupings: Party Youth Group, ages seventeen to twenty-five (although some 4 percent are past this age); the Vanguard Group, eleven to seventeen; and the Children's Organization, eight to eleven.

The Ho Chi Minh Communist Youth Group is organized parallel to the Lao Dong Party with the same organizational structure, from central committee (nineteen members) to local chapters. First secretary of the group since 1968 has been Vu Quang, also a national assemblyman from Hanoi and a frequent traveler abroad to international youth meetings. The group's secretariat consists of a five-member executive committee (equivalent of the Politburo) and eleven departments, each headed by a deputy group secretary.[7] The secretariat, whose members are appointed, is more powerful than the elected central committee. The Youth Group leadership is composed almost entirely of retired military officers and, in fact, Youth Groups at all levels are for the most part managed by retired military.

All youths in the movement get some form of military or paramilitary training. All are required to do what is called socially useful labor, usually involving public sanitation. And all are charged with internal security duties, that is, reporting suspected counterrevolutionary activity, including that of their parents.

A typical Ho Chi Minh Communist Youth Group at the basic or operational level consists of 120 boys and girls divided into four chapters of 30 members each, in turn divided into 15-person subchapters. The group is administered, under local adult Party supervision, by a seven-person executive committee (a secretary, the key figure; two deputies; and four members). Each chapter below the group is managed by a three-person executive committee (secretary, deputy, and agitprop cadre). Membership is by application, which must include two group members' letters of recommendation. The application is processed at the district level during a three-month waiting period. Then follows a six-month probation after which membership is granted. At age twenty-five, the group member is retired in a special ceremony, then usually joins the Party. The group has its own insignia (worn on the shirt), flag, song, and membership card. Competition within groups is encouraged. Attendance is required at the meetings, which are frequent, averaging about thirteen a month (one group meeting, four chapter meetings, and eight subchapter meetings).

The Ho Chi Minh Vanguard Youth Group, the next age level, traces its ancestry back to May 15, 1941, to what originally was called the Red Children's Group (Hong Nhi), which became, successively, the Vanguard Teenager Group, the National Salvation Teenager Group, the Young Pioneers, and finally in 1970, the Ho Chi Minh Vanguard Youth Group. In an average village (or city ward) a Vanguard chapter numbers around 300, divided into four or more teams, each of which is divided into twelve-person subteams. There is no hierarchy at this level and affairs are administered by the parent Ho Chi Minh Communist Youth Group executive committee. Membership is accomplished simply by administration of an oath. Dues are half that of the older youth organization. The Vanguard Youth Group has its own flag, insignia, and neck scarf emblazoned with a bamboo shoot.

For the youngest group there is the Ho Chi Minh Children's Organization (sometimes the Ho Chi Minh August Children's Organization), formerly the August Children's Group and before that the Children's National Salvation Group (sometimes referred to as the Children's Scout Group, or Dong Tu Quan). The unit here is the village or ward, usually organized by school class and averaging some 400 members. They wear a special insignia, a yellow star with a red eight in its center, and activity consists mainly of participating in public ceremonies and other local special events.

The Party's youth apparat is strongest, in fact only actually exists, at the basic level, the village or city ward. Here, at its best, it is a highly activist, energetic, and militant instrument supporting Party policies and programs.

In the South, before victory, a more praetorian Party structure existed for the young. It was called the Assault Youth Group and was a continuation of an institution founded by Ho Chi Minh in 1950 as part of the Viet Minh organizational forces. These groups were the local Party's paramilitary element. Members engaged in armed propaganda activities and guard duty and, in areas with PAVN units, acted as logistic and support troops. Many operated only part-time. The Assault Youth Group was open to those sixteen to thirty years old. Organizationally, it was divided into groups or companies (thirty-six to forty-eight persons), subdivided into squads or chapters (twelve persons) and then into three-man cells. Higher echelons, at provincial, regional, and national level, were an integral part of the adult Party organization. Basic-level administration or command was standard Party arrangement: a committee with a secretary and two deputies (operations and administration), plus specialized cadres, all under close adult Party control. Indoctrination efforts were more intense in the South, disciplinary measures more severe, awards and commendations more common and prestigious.

The Ho Chi Minh Communist Youth Group, as of late 1976, had an estimated membership of three million (vs. 800,000 in 1961), of whom about 280,000 had "cadre" status, meaning they had met minimal requirements in behavior and performance. The full-time Youth Group cadre corps, that is Party cadres assigned to youth affairs, was made up of about 13,500, of whom about 3,500 were working in the South.

FOURTH PARTY CONGRESS

After repeated delays, the Fourth Party Congress was staged in Hanoi December 14–20, 1976. A total of 1,008 delegates together with observers from twenty-nine foreign Communist parties, was in attendance.[8]

Out of the congress came a new leadership list, a series of organizational changes, and a new Party line, or ideological directive. The congress was no major turning point in Vietnam's history, but neither was it simply a morale-boosting celebration to put the frosting on the cake of victory in war. It offered no new programs or policies but did sharpen the focus of existing ones. It moved some already important officials into even more important positions but did not face up to the problem of generational transfer of power. It smoothed over but did not solve a variety of doctrinal disputes. Chiefly, the congress represented a declaration of Party centrality. The Party indicated it was and intended to remain Vietnam's dominant institution, source of all inspiration, fountain of all wisdom, monopolizer of all power. There was not to be in Vietnam, as was whispered about the USSR and Eastern Europe, any "irrelevancy" of the Party.

The Party's ruling organ, the Central Committee and Politburo, was enlarged, a reflection of absorption of the southern apparat, and existing vacancies were filled. The Politburo was expanded to 17 seats (14 plus 3 alternates). With 2 vacancies due to death and 1 due to retirement (Hoang Van Hoan), there were 7 new members joining the Politburo.[9] The Central Committee was nearly doubled, to 133 members

(101 regular plus 32 alternates). At least half of the Third Congress Central Committee were not on the new list, having died or been dropped or retired.

The congress approved a revision of Party structure. This involved amending Party bylaws, creating a single, all-Vietnam Communist party, and launching another campaign to improve the quality of cadres and members.

The obvious chief need in redrafting the bylaws was to incorporate the previously separate southern Party element. The Southern Branch arrangement had developed during the Viet Minh War largely for administrative reasons. This was changed in 1963, partly for administrative and partly for cosmetic reasons, to the more distinct People's Revolutionary Party. At the same time the Central Office (COSVN), which had been around in one form or another for the previous decade, developed increased authority. By the mid-1960s the COSVN and the PRP Central Committee were virtually synonymous. Gradually the PRP as a separate entity began to fade and the Party in the South became simply the Southern Organization (Dang Bo Mien Nam), a terminology that became more or less formal after take-over of the South. The new bylaws allow for incorporation of the southern members with respect to such all-important matters as Party age, or seniority.

The amended bylaws fix tougher standards for admission to the Party and for advancing through the ranks. They also tighted Party discipline, a move aimed at increasing unity and heading off factionalism.

The Fourth Congress changed the Party's name from the Vietnam Workers Party to the Vietnam Communist Party, ending a usage that began in 1951. The title of the leading Party official also was changed. The position of chairman was abolished and the title of first secretary, now the principal officer, became secretary general, also a return to an earlier usage.

Officially fixing Party membership at 1.56 million meant that previous estimates by outsiders of the size of the apparat in the South had been consistently low. Previous to the congress the Party in the North had numbered about one million (the range of estimates was from 200,000 to 950,000) and this, based on Politburo-level statements, can be considered firm. This means that the Party in the South, which had been estimated at no higher than 180,000, actually numbered at least 350,000 and may have had as many as 500,000 members.

FOREIGN RELATIONS

Communist Vietnam is now a major power in Asia. It has one of the largest and most effective military forces anywhere in the world.

The long-range goal of the Party and the new Socialist Republic of Vietnam (SRV) probably is creation of a Federation of Indochina, composed of Vietnam, Laos, and Cambodia. In the shorter run, the next decade or so, it will seek to shape these three countries into a loosely structured, confederated arrangement, one in which there is mutual advantage to all three and in which Vietnam is the first among equals. Gradually, the Vietnamese would hope, this structure would become institutionalized. Eventually would come full federation. To achieve this goal, the Vietnamese must overcome two major forces—historical fear and dislike on the part of the non-Vietnamese involved and the competition offered by the PRC and perhaps others.

The Party for years was successful in using the Sino-Soviet dispute to advantage, playing one side off the other, something no other country was able to do. This effort no longer is so successful. As noted earlier, the Party long has been irritated by the dispute and the international condition it was spawned, that is, détente and the erosion of proletarian international solidarity. These two effects have long been regarded as a reciprocal function. But both détente and the Sino-Soviet dispute appear to be conditions with which the Vietnamese must live for the foreseeable future.

Relations with the PRC and the USSR probably will be maintained on a bristly, independent, formally correct level, with the Vietnamese mostly following and not attempting to lead events. Relations with the PRC quite likely will be punctuated by hostile incidents.

Economic factors will condition external relations to a large degree, which means that prospects for outside aid will shape Vietnamese external behavior. The end of the war also ended Vietnamese dependence on its two allies for vitally needed war materials and weapons. But the two allies still are needed for economic assistance. The USSR has the greatest potential leverage here.

In general, the Vietnamese can be expected to play the role of the somewhat unfriendly loner, seeking no close alliances with any country and, in the conduct of foreign relations, being rigid and intransigent.

They will tend to be their own worst enemy, finding it difficult to overcome their psychological self-conditioning (once their greatest strength), which senses potential hostility everywhere, including where it does not exist, such as in Southeast Asia. Probably the Vietnamese Communists will not engage in what might be called old-fashioned aggression—the dispatch of tanks across international boundaries—but it will encourage those moves, including revolutionary warfare, that push various countries of the world toward becoming people's republics.

WINDS OF CHANGE

The Party's behavior over the years, both externally and internally, was marked by great continuity and steadfast purpose. Some call it fanaticism. Without doubt, historically the DRV was more constant in purpose, more consistent in action, than any other nation in modern times. Nor, for reasons not clear, was it buffeted by the winds of change as were other countries of the world, Communist and non-Communist alike.

This leads one to conclude that, in Vietnam, what is past is indeed prologue. Particularly as long as present leaders remain, the DRV, now the SRV, can be counted on to behave in a manner highly consistent with past behavior, to react as it has reacted, to choose as courses of action essentially straight-line continuations of previous courses without radical innovation or abrupt policy changes.

The most dynamic aspect of the Party at this writing is the matter of political succession. The present leadership is old. The average age of the Politburo in 1976 was sixty-six; the Central Committee, sixty-five. There is a generation gap, almost a two-generation gap, between the leaders and the rank and file. There are few transitional figures, and little is being done to groom younger persons (or even middle-aged individuals) for eventual top leadership.

This matter of the transfer of the mantle of power from the old generation to the new is one all countries must face periodically. In some the transition is orderly; in others, traumatic and even anarchical. There never is any sure way of knowing which it will be. In Vietnam, it is clear only that the leap will be a long one. A PAVN general who defected to the South during the war, when asked by the author about the question of political succession, replied: "You must remember Ho Chi Minh had no sons, he had only grandsons." We do not know what the grandsons will do when they come to power, but we do know from an examination of history that their way will not be grandfather's way. When the generational transfer of power comes in Vietnam, we can predict it will bring change, possibly drastic change, even though we do not know the direction that it will take.

What can be done at this time is to make a few observations about the nature of the future Vietnamese rulers. The author, during the 1960s, did research among PAVN prisoners of war and *hoi chanh* in the thirty-to-forty-year age bracket and found two general characteristics:

* Loyalty and devotion to the Vietnamese Communist system, but with strong pragmatic overtones. Not a single individual interviewed disapproved of the general Party cause—unification. Almost all, however, felt there were distinct limits to the sacrifice required to achieve this goal. Unlike their leaders (Ho Chi Minh: "No price is too high to pay"), they felt there was indeed too high a price for unification. When probed about their future goals, the response was almost uniform: raise the material level of life in Vietnam by socialist/communist means.

* A high level of idealism that, for persons in their third decade of life, bordered on naïveté. Particularly when compared with South Vietnamese, the generation that is to someday rule Vietnam exhibited an uncommon credulity. Quite probably this was the result of their carefully contained education and their almost total isolation from the influence of disruptive ideas from the outside. They knew little about the world and its ways. They had enormous faith in the perfectibility of man and the possibilities of creating a problemless society. In a teenager, this is understandable and common, but not in a Vietnamese in his thirties. This idealism was a great strength during the war years. It could be a great weakness in a leadership that becomes battered by disillusionment.

During the 1970s, and particularly after victory in the South, persistent and reliable reports out of Hanoi told of a growing gulf between younger and older Party cadres, often described as a demand by young cadres to liberate the Party from "old guardism." As a youth-age issue, it is not, of course, uncommon. The cutting edge of the difference appeared to be ideological orthodoxy, that is, the question of how far an ideology can be bent without breaking it. Generally, the young stood for ideological liberalism, that is, flexible interpretation of doctrine, while the old guard was more conservative. Also involved was the matter of communist internationalism and proletarian solidarity. Here, unexpectedly perhaps, the young demonstrated isolationism, rejecting to some degree the notion of solidarity and tending instead to view internationalism as merely a covert means by which outsiders (that is, the USSR and the PRC) manipulate domestic Vietnamese affairs.

The eventual new leaders, whoever they are, can be expected to carry these characteristics. Also, quite likely, they will be Party generalists, not educated sons of gentry, not peasant generals, not technocrats.

While the present leaders remain, it is likely that their present operational code of decision making also will remain: the agreement to disagree, collective unanimous decisions, no preeminent individual leader. If one key member dies or becomes incapacitated, the operational code may come apart; if three or more key members go, the odds rise from possible to probable. In any event, political succession is only a matter of time, perhaps not a great deal of time.

The major problems the leaders of the new unified Socialist Republic of Vietnam will face, and the determinants of their success as rulers, will be fourfold. The first will be economic, central to which is development of a rational agricultural system with vastly increased productivity; this against the starkest present statistic: 85 percent of the labor force is engaged in feeding the total population, yet 20 percent of the rice eaten must be imported. The approach to this problem probably will be Maoist, that is, emphasis on motivation and nonmaterial appeals.

The second problem will be internal security, mainly in connection with incorporating the South into the system in a manner that does not drive the southerners into desperate widespread resistance. Third will be foreign relations, working out some new formula for dealing with the USSR, the probably troublesome Chinese, the other Indochinese countries, the Southeast Asian countries, and, finally, the rest of the world. For the first time, actually, the Vietnamese Communists are obliged to face outward.

Finally, there is the problem of ideology. A terrible centrifugal force will be at work with which the leadership must cope, including the insidious notion of the "irrelevance" of the Party.

The Party's obsession with unification over the decades buried a negative dimension of this golden dream. There can be debilitation in absorption. Assimilation of the South—that vastly differing society with its stubborn, entrenched divisiveness—ironically could prove to be the self-inflicted act that destroyed the system's greatest strength, its monolithic nature. Vietnam could move unknowingly and imperceptibly from one state of existence to another, from a solidly unified society to simply one more schizoid country with built-in, dividing weakness. Such, at least, is the challenge future leaders face, although at this writing it is only a small cloud on the horizon.

For two traumatic decades, Communist Vietnam curiously escaped the winds of change that buffeted the rest of the world. Events were frozen in the war. Now, it is clear, the clock has begun to run again in Vietnam. Time has started moving in its erosive, mysterious way. Change is about to assault the society and the Party. Time and change are what Vietnam will now be all about.

Notes

1. THE BIRTH OF VIETNAMESE COMMUNISM

1. Histories of the Vietnamese Communist movement are remarkably scarce considering the world attention the Party has received in recent years. The Party itself, since 1960, has published a Party history every five years, essentially revising the 1960 version (see the Dang Lao Dong entry in the Bibliography). I. Milton Sacks, P. J. Honey, the late Bernard B. Fall, and Hoang Van Chi were early students of Vietnamese communism and produced useful but not extensive works. The only full-scale recent history of the Party by a non-Vietnamese is Robert F. Turner's *Vietnamese Communism,* which also contains valuable appendixes. William J. Duiker, Carlyle A. Thayer, and William S. Turley are younger students of Vietnamese communism who have done some excellent and resourceful work, but apparently none is able to devote himself full-time to the subject, there not being much of a professional career to be carved out in this field. General works on Vietnam include some extensive discussions of Vietnamese communism. See especially the writings of Robert Shaplen, Dennis J. Duncanson, Paul Mus, Donald Lancaster, Joseph Buttinger, Denis Warner, George McKahin, and John T. McAlister and the works of various French writers listed in the Bibliography.

2. For discussion of early political movements predating communism in Vietnam, see writings of Alexander B. Woodside (early nineteenth century), David G. Marr (late nineteenth century), and William J. Duiker (early twentieth century); see also Ngo Vinh Long.

3. At the time, known as Nguyen Ai Quoc. For a discussion of Ho's names and aliases, see chap. 4, note 1.

4. In 1919 some sixty communist parties throughout the world formed an organization headquartered in Moscow called the Third International or, commonly, the Comintern (later, in somewhat changed form, the Cominform). Its proclaimed objective was world revolution through furthering the communist cause everywhere. For discussion of the Comintern and Vietnamese Communism see Charles B. McLane, *Soviet Strategies in Southeast Asia,* and William J. Duiker, *The Comintern and Vietnamese Communism.*

5. From the official party history, Dang Lao Dong, *Thirty-five Years of Struggle of the Party,* p. 3. Neither this nor other official histories list the ICP founders. From scattered references it appears that the youths joining with Ho included Pham Van Dong, Tran Van Cung, Nguyen Duc Canh, Le Hong Phong, Ho Tung Mau, and as the sixth man either Le Hong Son, Ngo Gia Tu, or Lam Duc Thu. Official histories suggest, but do not state, that Nguyen Luong Bang and Hoang Van Hoan were founders; this is unlikely.

6. The residue groups of the Tan Viet, which included (in earlier form) the Vietnam Revolutionary Party and the Vietnam Revolutionary League; at times these groups, or elements of them, went under the banner of Vietnam Restoration. Early leaders, many of whom appear later in the Communist movement, included Duy Dao Anh, Le Duy Diem, Ton Quang Phiet, Nguyen Si Sach, and Tran Phu.

7. Early writers of the Vietnam scene, French as well as others, ascribe more zeal or fanaticism to central (that is, Annamese) Vietnamese Communists than to Tonkinese or Cochin Chinese, some even centering the early Communist movement entirely in the central Vietnam (Hue) region. See, for example. Thomas E. Ennis, *French Policy and Developments in Indochina,* Appendix E, "The General Features of Communism in Indochina."

8. Dang Lao Dong, *Thirty-five Years,* pp. 27–29.

9. The Comintern directive of October 27, 1929, ordering formation of the ICP was published by *Nhan dan,* January 6, 1970. See also Tran Phu (or Tran Phu Thao), "Political thesis," *Quan doi nhan dan,* January 5, 1970.

10. For a listing of the conditions see Sidney Hook, ed., *World Communism: Key Documentary Material* (New York: Van Nostrand, 1962).

11. Initially there was an additional level in the hierarchy, the Chinese Communist Party Central Committee, sandwiched between the Far Eastern Bureau and Moscow. This level was eliminated in the early 1930s.

12. Dang Lao Dong, *Forty-five Years of Activities of the Dang Lao Dong,* p. 104.

13. Dang Lao Dong, *Thirty Years of Struggle of the Party,* p. 62.

14. Ibid., p. 44.

15. February 3, 1930, is the official Indochinese Communist Party founding date, although some Hanoi publications (such as *Thu do,* February 3, 1963) state, "The Party was founded by Ho Chi Minh and six others in March 1929"). March 3, 1951, is officially listed as the day the ICP changed its name to the Dang Lao Dong (Workers Party). See *Vietnam fact book* (Hanoi: Pho Thong Publishing House, 1970). As the ICP, Party activity during the 1930s also

included Laos and Cambodia. The ICP founded the Laos Regional Party Committee in 1930 (and chapters in the next three years in Vientiane, Savannakhet, Thakhet, and Pakse); Party activity in Cambodia in the 1930s apparently was administered by the Cochin Chinese Regional Party Central Committee.

16. Dang Lao Dong, *Forty-five Years,* p. 59.

2. THE 1930s: CHALLENGE AND FRUSTRATION

1. Dang Lao Dong, *Thirty Years,* p. 16.

2. Quoted in Joseph Buttinger, *The Dragon Embattled* (New York: Praeger Publishers, 1967), 1: 557.

3. It should be understood that, even so, this was revolution in microcosm. ICP strength was not more than 1,500, with a total collaborating force (that is Nationalists, front groups, etc.) of less than 100,000. Ranged against this were some 11,000 French army regulars, 16,000 Indochinese militia (which served at the provincial level under the provincial French resident as units made up of French officers, including French foreign legionnaires, and Vietnamese enlisted men with responsibility for pacification of their provinces), and some 500 French Surete agents. This was for all of Indochina. The entire French *colon* population during the 1930s (official and unofficial; men, women, and children) was less than 42,000. Only a fraction of the forces on both sides was actually engaged in militancy or combat during the 1930 outbreak of violence.

4. Primarily in the districts of Thanh Chuong, Huong Son, Nam Dan, Hung Nguyen, Hong Son, and Nghi Loc.

5. Dang Lao Dong, *Thirty Years,* p. 34.

6. Secretary General Tran Phu wrote a critique titled "Theses on the bourgeois democratic revolution in Vietnam." The Comintern (June 1932) asked for and got a policy statement, "ICP action program," which, drawing from Phu's report, incorporated the Comintern view of what it considered improper Party policy guidance in Vietnam.

7. These are VNQDD figures and may be inflated.

8. See Dennis J. Duncanson, "Ho Chi Minh in Hong Kong, 1931–32," *China Quarterly,* 1975, no. 1, pp. 84–100.

9. Organizational activity was divided into three categories: *legal* activity was open support of, including membership in, an organization that stood for some purpose the Party could accept, for example, a women's rights group; *semilegal* activity was work within an organization that could be used or turned to Party benefit, for example, a trade union or a veterans group; *illegal* (or covert) activity was the hidden or secret manipulation of an organization, often against its own interests, for example, pushing a student or youth group into militant action that brought reprisals by the French. The legal struggle came into its own with the emergence of the Popular Front in 1936.

10. Called *khoi nghia* in Vietnamese. This was a social myth (in the Sorelian sense) akin to the industrialized communist's social myth of the general strike. For detailed discussion of this see Douglas Pike, *General Uprising: The Viet Cong's Durable Social Myth*. (Saigon: U.S. Mission, 1972).

11. Under the generic term *Popular Front* the Party in Indochina formed a series of front organizations: the Antiimperialist People's Front (mid-1936); the All-Indochina Front (early 1937); the Indochinese Democratic Front (early 1938); and the Indochinese Democratic Unified (or United) Front (later in 1938).

12. The communist nature (or *style* is perhaps a better term) of the VNQDD organizations continued in an unbroken line for the next twenty-five years, to the last significant movement in which its members were involved: the Can Lao, formed by Ngo Dinh Nhu (President Ngo Dinh Diem's brother), which was communist in structure (cell/central committee), semicovert, and Marxist in its language and philosophical outlook (historical determinism), even while being militantly anti-communist.

13. As an émigré group in China, it splintered in the 1930s. The so-called Kunming faction, under Vu Hong Khang, emerged as the dominant successor. The Dai Viet Quoc Dan Dang (Greater Vietnam Nationalist Party) was formed in Hanoi out of the remnants of the original VNQDD movement there and became something of a local force during the next several decades. Also to be noted, as part of this first stream of Vietnamese Nationalists, was the Viet Nam Cach Mang Dong Minh Hoi (Vietnam Revolutionary League), usually called the Dong Minh Hoi, (not to be confused with the Phuc Quoc Dong Minh Hoi, usually called the Phuc Quoc (discussed below). The Dong Minh Hoi was formed in China under Chinese patronage (its leader, Nguyen Hai Than, was also a general in the Nationalist Chinese army) and returned to Vietnam after World War II. Poor behavior by the occupying KMT troops ruined the Dong Minh Hoi, since it was closely associated with the KMT. Elements of it, however, continued active in various organizational structures during the next decade.

14. The prince died in 1951, never having returned to Vietnam. Many Phuc Quoc leaders and rank and file joined the Cao Dai and Hoa Hao sects (discussed below).

15. Sometimes translated as "Go East movement." It began after the Japanese victory over Russia in 1905.

16. The Dai Viet movement began in the early 1930s as a breakaway VNQDD group. Initially it consisted of two elements, the Dai Viet Duy Dan (Greater Advancement of the People) and the Dai Viet Quoc Xa (Greater Socialism). The former was more mainstream; the latter, under Nguyen Van Tieu (or Rua) was a semifascist, elitist, pro-Japanese group. By the late 1930s the Dai Viet Quoc Dan Dang had emerged from this initial division and consisted of three streams: (1) the Revolutionary Dai Viet (Dai Viet Cach Mang) under Ha Thuc Ky, chiefly in central Vietnam; (2) the New Dai Viet (Tan Dai Viet) under Nguyen Ngoc

Huy; and (3) the Orthodox Dai Viet (Dai Viet Chinh Thong) under Tran Van Xuan. Ky now lives in Washington, D.C.; Huy, in San Diego, California; and Xuan died in Saigon in 1971.

17. Truong Chinh, *President Ho Chi Minh,* p. 34.

18. Portions of the documents were published in *Quan doi nhan dan,* January 24, 1970.

19. Details were described to me by Do Quang Giai, the last non-Communist mayor of Hanoi.

3. WORLD WAR II: OPPORTUNITY

1. *Vietnam Courier,* February 1970; reprinted as *Landmarks in Party History* Hanoi, ?).

2. The directive was printed clandestinely as a pamphlet (n.d.) and distributed at the time.

3. Party historians maintain that nine of every ten prisoners in Japanese jails in Indochina during World War II were Party members.

4. Dang Lao Dong, *Thirty Years,* p. 3. The initial force consisted of three platoons, whose commanders were Vo Nguyen Giap (alias Col. Nam), Van Tien Dung, and Chu Van Tan, the DRV's military big three of the next two decades.

5. A Bao Dai government had been formed by the Japanese around Prime Minister Tran Trong Kim on April 7, 1945.

6. This is a questionable statistic, one based on USSR reportage at the time. It is questionable whether any statistical count was (or could have been) taken at the time. No doubt thousands perished, weakened by malnutrition.

7. According to Vo Nguyen Giap's memoirs, *Unforgettable Days,* p. 79, this moment (August 1945) was the first time Ho Chi Minh (aged fifty-five) had ever set foot in Hanoi.

8. For a discussion of this see Douglas Pike, *Viet Cong,* pp. 27–28, 45–46.

4. LEADERSHIP

1. An explanatory note on Ho Chi Minh's names and aliases: His first or "sacred" name, given to him by his parents at birth, was Nguyen Van Cung (*cung,* sometimes spelled *coong,* meaning respectful). As was the custom in old Vietnam, at about the age of ten Ho was permitted to choose (or was given) his "real" name, which has variously been reported as Nguyen Tat Thanh, Nguyen That Thanh, and Nguyen Van Thanh, with the first now the most generally accepted; it, like those which followed, were poetic, *tat thanh* meaning inevitable success. In his early twenties he assumed Nguyen Ai Quoc (*ai quoc* meaning love of country, or patriot). When he returned to Vietnam in 1945 it was as Ho Chi Minh (*minh* meaning enlightenment, or one who shines)—according to some

Vietnamese this name was given to him by his Chinese jailers as *shedder of light,* a reaction to his penchant for lecturing them). In the intervening years he used a host of aliases—many of them puns in Vietnamese or Chinese—including Nguyen O Phap (Francophobe), Ly Thuy, Vuong Son Nhi, Song Man Cho (Sung Meng Chiao), Sinh Chin, Lee Swee (in Hong Kong), Golin (Paris), Linov (Soviet Union), Ba (nickname used when messboy on a French liner), Old Chen and Old Tran (at age fifty in China), Nilovsky, and Truong Nhuoc Trung.

2. At least three "official" biographies of Ho have been produced by the Party (see Bibliography), the most authoritative, perhaps, being Truong Chinh's *President Ho Chi Minh.* At least short biographical sketches of Ho have been produced by virtually all top Party leaders, including Le Duan, Pham Van Dong, and Vo Nguyen Giap. Ho never wrote an autobiography, although his four-volume *Selected Works: 1929–60* contains several biographical sketches, for example, his essay "The Path which Led me to Leninism." Biographies have been written by numerous outsiders, including Charles Fenn, Jean Lacouture, Nguyen Khac Huyen, Jean Sainteny, David Halberstam, and William Warbey. The most recent is my own "Ho Chi Minh: A Postwar Reevaluation" (Paper delivered at the Thirty-first Orientalist Congress, Mexico City, 1976).

3. Respectively, in Vietnamese, the Hoi Lien Hiep Cac Dan Toc Thuoc Dia and the Nhom Nguoi Viet Nam Yeu Nuoc. The Intercolonial Union often is encountered in literature of the period as the League of Colored Peoples.

4. Len an chu nghia de quoc Phap [Condemnation of French imperialism], published in 1920 and revised (reportedly with major help from Nguyen The Truyen) and published in French in 1925 as *Le procès de le colonisation française.* In it Ho rewrote Lenin's thesis on national and colonial questions, called for an alliance between Western urban proletariat and native colonials (on a tutor-pupil basis), outlined plans for a pan-Asian federation that would be a coequal participant in the worldwide proletarian revolution, and, most of all, provided Vietnamese political émigrés in Paris with their own political bible.

5. See Duncanson, "Ho Chi Minh in Hong Kong."

6. See Duiker, *Comintern and Vietnamese Communism.*

7. Vo Nguyen Giap, "Uncle Ho's heart," *Van hoa nghe thuat,* December 1972, p. 41.

8. Quoted by Ta Quang Buu, "Uncle Ho and science," *To quoc,* August 1970, p. 12.

9. *Nhan dan,* September 5, 1969.

10. Truong Chinh, *President Ho Chi Minh,* p. 112.

11. Leadership below this top level was composed mainly of ex–French regime civil servants and village gentry. Few were proletarian. Bernard Fall studied DRV leadership circa 1953 and found that of 1,850 Party cadres in key positions, 73 percent had bourgeoisie background (i.e., middle-class or professional/intellectual), 19 percent were peasant/gentry, and 8 percent urban proletarian. Formal education appears to have been somewhat less important a

factor among the leadership at this level, although almost all were well-trained revolutionaries, having been educated for the most part in jail. (*Le Viet Minh, 1945–60.* p. 74).

5. VIET MINH WAR: CRUCIBLE YEARS

1. See Bernard Fall, *Viet Minh,* for details of the 1946 constitution.

2. See King C. Chen, *Vietnam and China;* also, Turner, *Vietnamese Communism.*

3. Fall discusses French Communists and Indochina in "Solution in Indochina," *Foreign Affairs,* April 1955.

4. French casualties in the Viet Minh War (December 1945–July 1954): Killed, dead, or missing, 92,707; wounded, 76,369. Breakdown by nationality (combined figures for dead, missing, and wounded): metropolitan French, 20,685; foreign legion, 11,620; African troops, 29,000; Indochinese in French army, 27,163; Indochinese in Vietnamese provincial force, 17,597. After the war the Viet Minh released 19,221 prisoners; there remained unaccounted for another 30,861 (21,861 French and 9,000 Indochinese). The Viet Minh never released its casualty figures.

5. Dang Lao Dong, *Brief history of our Party and eight lessons of experience,* p. 19.

6. Party histories published in recent years indicate that the Party continued to operate exactly as before, still under the ICP banner. See discussion of Ho's arguments for "withdrawing into secrecy" by Thanh Dam, "Understanding the three Party Congresses," *Nghien cuu lich su,* September–October 1976.

7. Initially, however, the Left Bank was not much of a government. In 1945, in an act of demagoguery (or naïveté), it abolished all taxation, hoping to survive on customs levies and donations. It soon found itself with a starving population and a bankrupt administration. See Donald Lancaster, *The Emancipation of French Indochina,* for details of administration in the Viet Minh zone.

8. The Dai Viets were influential during this period in non–Viet Minh areas of Tonkin, chiefly through members who were civil servants in the National Popular movement (or, in Cochin China, the Younger Patriot movement), led by one Le Thang.

9. See Philippe Devillers, *Histoire du Vet Nam de 1940 à 1952.*

10. U.S., Department of State, *Working Papers on North Vietnam's Role in the War in South Vietnam,* no. 211, p. 171. Nos. 2 and 211 of the *Working Papers* carry the Second Party Congress documents. See also Allan B. Cole, *Conflict in Indochina and International Repercussions* (Ithaca: Cornell University Press, 1956), and Robert Turner, *Vietnamese Communism,* appendixes.

11. U.S., Department of State, *Working Papers on North Vietnam's Role,* no. 211, p. 112.

12. The semantic changes gave the Party group trouble. They were defended in a 1951 Party memorandum, which argued that *worker* is a better term than *communist* for "completing the task of liberating" the nation; it cited precedent

(Poland, Hungary, Korea), and it noted that "later when conditions are favorable . . . we will readopt the name Communist Party" (ibid., p. 117).

13. Dang Lao Dong, *Brief history of our Party*, p. 92.

14. See discussion of Geneva Conference in Douglas Pike, *War, Peace, and the Viet Cong*.

15. Discussed in detail in Pike, *Viet Cong*.

6. THE PARTY IN POWER

1. Bernard Fall, in *Viet Minh*, compares the 1946 and 1960 constitutions. The former bore a closer relationship to the PRC's, the latter to the USSR's. A few non-Communists were in the new government. For example, Hoang Minh Giam, a Socialist, was foreign minister at a time when there were few foreign relations; a week before the 1954 Geneva Conference he mysteriously took "sick" and was replaced by a trusted Party official, Ung Van Khiem. In practice the Party covered a ministry run by a non-Communist with a special representative. Thus the minister of health, Dr. Ton That Tung, had a deputy, Dr. Pham Ngoc Thach, prominent Saigon Party member. Catholic Minister of Economy Nguyen Manh Ha attempted to oppose Party leaders on economic programs, then abandoned the government and departed for France.

2. The title of the chief Party official was changed from secretary general to first secretary, indicative, according to some observers, of a shift from Chinese to USSR Communist Party influence.

3. Operation Exodus, according to the records of the international organizations involved, saw the transfer of 727,000 persons from North to South; the GVN said the figure eventually reached one million. About 60 percent were Catholic. At the same time, some 50,000 persons (90,000 according to Communist sources) went from South to North. Almost all of those who went North came out of three central Vietnam provinces, Binh Dinh, Phu Yen, and Quang Ngai.

4. This organ, also known as the Central Office (later appearing as COSVN—Central Office of South Vietnam) was composed of six members: Le Duan, Le Duc Tho, Pham Hung, Ha Huy Giap, Truong Vu, and Ung Van Khiem. A seven-page Party document dated November 1951 detailing the creation of the Central Office as well as other internal Party developments of the period is contained in U.S., Department of State, *Working Papers on North Vietnam's Role*, no. 2.

5. In mid-1956 the Diem government launched a Denunciation of Communist Subversion campaign, which was designed to root out remaining Party and subversive elements by soliciting information from local villagers. In 1959 the GVN reported to the International Control Commission (ICC) that some 15,000 North Vietnamese agents had been identified and 3,561 caches of arms and ammunition uncovered.

6. Methods to induce turnover of businesses included excessive taxation, denial of credit, and access to raw materials, imposition of impossible price controls, and, occasionally, outright confiscation or use of terror. Harsher measures were used against the comprador bourgeois ("Those who chiefly were distributors of French goods or contractors of public works," that is, with direct affiliation with the French) and lesser measures against the national bourgeois (defined as "those who tried to develop the national economy but met with strong opposition from the colonial administration and thus nurtured aspirations of independence"). The line between the comprador and the national bourgeois was never made clear. Later, *national bourgeois* was defined as "former exploiters"; gradually the status was eliminated. ([Democratic Republic of Vietnam], *A Century of Struggles,* Vietnam Studies no. 24, p. 12. See also Edwin E. Moise, "Land Reform and Land Reform Errors in North Vietnam," *Pacific Affairs,* December 1975.)

7. Collectivization began at the Party's Second Congress, in 1950, which announced a two-stage program for the rural areas: (a) redistribute the land, chiefly to the landless (*ban co*) so as to restructure the rural class system (Pham Van Dong later said ths stage was completed by February 1958); (b) collectivize the agricultural sector into large cooperatives/communes. The official view was that this program had a fivefold accomplishment: the feudal landlord class was eliminated; individual ownership of land was abolished; some two million families received land; the old sociopolitical structure of the village was destroyed; a worker-peasant alliance was formed.

The name of the institution employed changed over the years. Initially it was the work exchange team (or mutual exchange team or labor exchange brigade), a concept historically similar to the harvest team, but in Party hands a code word for collectivization. The term is still employed today, although *cooperative* is preferred. These are collectives and are far more similar to the Chinese commune than to, say, the American production or marketing farm-cooperative. In the early years, the work exchange team varied greatly from area to area. Some were marketing or production cooperatives. They had a capitalist base, that is, cooperative production but individual (or family) economic benefit. What was important, Party cadres insisted, was not the economic arrangement but the spirit of mutuality; cadres stressed collectiveness rather than class consciousness and gave the institution an orientation of spirit rather than ideology. In many instances Party cadres had no clear opinion of the work exchange team except as a means to increase food production. Whatever its psychic value, the program floundered organizationally. The number of teams declined after an auspicious start. In mid-1956, some 60 percent of all villages had work exchange teams; by the end of 1957 this had dropped to 22 percent; a new drive returned it to 43 percent (late 1958), then to 68 percent (spring of 1959), at which time it was phased into the collectivization program. The number of work exchange teams or collectives thus rose from 4,722 in 1958 to 41,410 (85 percent of all farm units) in 1960. In 1963 a consolidation program reduced the number of collectives to about 30,000 (incorporating 88 percent of all farm families. About a third of these, in the early 1960 period, were collectives termed *high* (as opposed to *low*). In high-level collectives, land, animals, and machinery are the property of the state, not the collective; the state invests capital to permit greater mechanization; individuals are salaried workers, their income based, not on share of production, but on a work-day point system; the product of the collective belongs to the state. In low-level collectives, members retain operational control of land, livestock, tools (even though title may have passed to the state); land is rented to the collective; each member helps farm communally; (a small percentage of the acreage, around 5 percent, is retained for "private plots" farmed by the family, which is free to dispose of the produce, usually vegetables, as it wishes); output is sold to the state at a predetermined fixed rate; proceeds are divided among members of the collective (with a size-of-household adjustment factor being incorporated). Inevitably, some collectives (or villages) tend to be richer than others (with no system for equalization at the local level), although rural-area income during this period was below that of the cities; the rural-urban income ratio reportedly was about 1:2. The Party response to this was to consolidate collectives, working toward the so-called super collective with some 50,000 farm workers each and with vast acreages of land put into diversified farming. These were foreshadowed by the development of the state farm system. By the mid-1960s, about fifty-five were in operation (thirty-three of them run by the PAVN), working a total of 200,000 hectares and employing some 60,000 agricultural workers.

8. Typical of the attitude is this passage from *The DRV on the Road to Socialist Industry* (Hanoi: FLPH, 1960): "To get rid of poverty and backwardness our foremost task is to industrialize our country. Only with the development of a large-scale industry can we guarantee the technical re-equipment of the whole of our national economy, including agriculture, raise labor productivity and the people's living standards."

9. *Proceedings of the Third Party Congress*, 3 vols. (Hanoi: FLPH, 1960), 1:112.

10. Of the five categories, the first two (class A and B) were the exploiter class; the remaining three (C, D, and E) were the exploited class. Specifically:

Class A: landlords (usually "dishonest and ferocious landlords"); owned but did not work land; often gentry, gentry-scholar or village elite

Class B: rich peasants (the "average, normal landlord"); owned land, part farmed by themselves and the remainder rented to tenants

Class C: middle peasants (or "richer peasants"); owned and worked land and sometimes leased part of it, but not as landlords (that is, did not provide normal landlord services)

Class D: poor peasants (or "strong middle-level peasants") either tenants or owned and worked their own land

Class E: landless peasants (or "very poor peasants" or agricultural workers); the *ban co,* "poor for many generations," class

11. Originally at least one trial per village (or hamlet) and later raised to five per village. The *Pentagon Papers* contain detailed citation, based chiefly on

northern-refugee testimony on the People's Agricultural Reform Tribunals. Bernard Fall wrote that 50,000 were executed and 100,000 sent to reform camps (*The Two Vietnams*, pp. 156–57). Other estimates vary above and below this.

12. He reported: "Cadres in carrying out the anti-feudal task created contradictions in the tasks of Land Reform and the (Cultural) Revolution. In some areas treating them as to separate activities. . . .

"We failed to recognize the need to achieve unity with the (Class C) middle-level peasants and should have formed an alliance with the (Class B) rich peasants instead of treating them as (Class A) landlords. . . .

"We attacked indiscriminately all families owning land. . . .

"We deviated from the purpose of the campaign with the result that many honest people were executed. We attacked indiscriminately, saw enemies everywhere, resorted to widespread terror. . . .

"We failed to respect religious freedom and right to freedom of worship in some areas in our effort to implement land reform. . . .

"We failed to respect the customs of the (Montagnard) tribes, and attacked too strongly their leaders and hierarchal system.

"In Party organization we placed too much emphasis on social class origin rather than political attitudes. Rather than to utilize education to improve Party member quality we resorted to administrative measures such as disciplinary punishment, dissolution of Party basic units, expulsion and execution of members. Worse still, torture came to be regarded as a normal part of Party reorganization. . . ." [*Realites vietnamiennes* (Paris), no. 3 (February 1957); this magazine carried the full text of Giap's "grave errors" speech.]

13. Truong Chinh was demoted (Ho Chi Minh replaced him as secretary general) but remained in the Central Committee and Politburo. Ho Viet Thang was expelled from the Central Committee but remained a Party member. Le Van Luong was removed from the Secretariat and the Politburo but remained an alternate member of the Central Committee. Both Thang (made chief villian) and Luong were fired from their various governmental posts.

14. Fall, *Two Vietnams* (which contains a detailed description of the Nghe An uprising), pp. 156–57.

7. UNIFICATION

1. Ho Chi Minh, *Selected Works: 1929–60*, 2: 102.

2. For a detailed description see Douglas Pike, *Viet Cong*.

3. The two Communist armed forces discussed in this chapter are the North Vietnamese armed force, called the People's Army of Vietnam (PAVN), and the People's Liberation Armed Force (PLAF), originally the Liberation Army, which was the armed force of the National Liberation Front of South Vietnam (and later of the Provisional Revolutionary Government, or PRG). The PAVN at this time consisted of about 420,000 men including about twelve infantry divisions (12,000 men each), a 3,000-man air force, and a 2,500-man navy. In

addition, the DRV had a 250,000-man Regional Militia Force and a 28,000-man quasi-military Armed Public Security Force. Backing up these regular and regional forces was a Self-Defense Force, a paramilitary organization of some three million men and women; members of SDF received military training, performed local security missions, and served as a backup reserve for the PAVN. The southern army, PLAF, was divided into two elements: the full military force (usually called main-force units) and the paramilitary (or guerrilla force, which was of two types: the regional or territorial guerrilla unit and the local guerrilla unit).

4. Vo Nguyen Giap, *Big Victory, Great Task.*

5. The decision to send PAVN forces in numbers to the South, it now seems reasonably clear, was made at a Party plenum in early 1964. Special six-week training sessions for this assignment—at the famed Xuan Mai infiltration camp outside Hanoi—began in the spring, and trainees entered the Ho Chi Minh trail in late summer. By the end of the year they were arriving in strength. This was two months before the American announcement that it was entering the war.

6. Clearly there was a major Communist buildup during 1972 and 1973. Combat strength increased from about 130,000 to 170,000 combat troops. The infiltration rate from North to South averaged about 15,000 per month (with the northward flow about 5,000). The tank inventory—T-54 medium tanks and T-34 light tanks—increased from 100 to 600; some 50 armored personnel carriers also were added. The number of large artillery pieces (122mm and 130mm guns) trebled. Twelve air fields were built in Communist-controlled areas, ten of them defended by surface-to-air missiles. Communist military strength at this time: the PAVN, 140,000 combat troops and 20,000 administrative troops; the PLAF, 30,000 full-military and 100,000 paramilitary (half of the latter being regional or territorial guerrillas and half local guerrillas); the PRG/NLF cadres, about 70,000.

7. See Pike, *War, Peace, and the Viet Cong,* pp. 148–57, for the continuum.

8. Had the Paris Agreement been scrupulously observed, the DRV would have had no way legally to support its 150,000 troops remaining in the South (the agreement made Laos, Cambodia, and the DMZ sacrosanct.)

9. Sen. Gen. Van Tien Dung, "Great Spring Victory," Foreign Broadcast Information Service (FBIS), April and May 1966.

10. Up to 80,000 experienced guerrillas (depending on which figures are accepted) were regrouped to the North under Le Duan's orders, being told at the time that they were to be trained for eventual return.

11. The first significant return was with the formation of the famed 559 Transportation Agency, responsible for traffic on what came to be called the Ho Chi Minh trail, formed in May 1959 (hence its name).

12. For biographical data on Vo Chi Cong as well as on other southern Party officials see Pike, *Viet Cong.*

13. Tracing Party leaders in the South during the Vietnam War is complicated by the presence of Tran Nam Trung. Possibly this was a position—*tran*

nam trung means loyal southerner—rather than an individual; or possibly it was both person and position. Over the years various high-level Party officials have been identified with this alias, including Pham Van Dang, Nguyen Van Linh, Nguyen Chi Thanh, and Tran Van Tra (all of whom employed other aliases if not this one). From 1961, with the departure of Huynh Van Tam, until the advent in 1965 of Nguyen Chi Thanh (who may have arrived earlier, as Tran Nam Trung), the top Party leader in the South either was Tran Nam Trung or one or more persons using that name. In the early 1970s some analysts insisted that Tran Nam Trung was and always had been Gen. Tran Van Tra. This was apparently disproven, however, when, at the May 1975 postwar celebration in Saigon, General Tra appeared on the reviewing stand alongside someone identified as Tran Nam Trung.

14. The 1960 Third Party Congress elected some ten "hidden" members to the Party Central Committee. Their names were not revealed because they were working in the South. Postwar appearances and assignments now make the identity of these Central Committee members reasonably certain: Nguyen Van Linh (alias Nguyen Van Cuc, etc.); Pham Van Dang (alias Pham Xuan Thai, etc.); Vo Chi Cong; Tran Nam Trung, whatever his true name; Nguyen Van Ho, the Party's financial and economic chief in the South; probably, Huynh Tan Phat, the PRG president; possibly, Le Van Kiet (alias Nguyen Van Kiet), who was (before being superseded by Nguyen Van Ho) the major (covert) Party official in Saigon.

8. THE PARTY TODAY

1. Which at this writing was still in a state of transition.

2. The translation of *xa hoi chu nghia* as *socialist* is somewhat puzzling. Normally in Vietnamese *socialist* is simply *xa hoi*, as in the Hanoi-based Radical Socialist Party (Dang Xa Hoi Cap Tien). The term *chu nghia* is comparable to the suffix *ism* in English (as in communism or socialism). Literally, therefore, the new name of Vietnam, Cong Hoa Xa Hoi Chu Nghia Vietnam should be translated as the Republic of Socialism of Vietnam. *Xa hoi chu nghia*, instead of simply *xa hoi*, is apparently used for some esoteric ideological reason.

3. Cited in the Douglas Pike, *Communist Party of South Vietnam* (which quotes, in part, Lao Dong Party Directive 31 CT/TW, June 4, 1957), p. 7.

4. The Party bylaws stipulate that the Central Committee be elected every four years. The 1960 election named forty-two regular members, thirty alternates, and ten unannounced, or "secret," members from the South. Sixteen of the forty-two were carry-overs from the 1950 congress.

5. Depending on whether the 1941 meeting that created the Viet Minh is also considered a Party congress.

6. Most of the organizational effort was handled by the group's patron saint, Ly (sometimes Le) Tu Trong who was born in Ha Tinh province, raised in Thailand, and joined Ho in Canton in the Thanh Nien days. He was the first

Youth Group leader and its first martyr when he was beheaded (at the age of nineteen) for assassinating a French Surete agent.

7. The executive committee, under Vu Quang, is composed of Nguyen Van Cam, Le Xuan Dong, Phan Thi Phuoc, Nguyen Thanh Duong, and Hoang Hoa. The eleven deputy secretaries are Ho Truc, Ta Quang Chien, Le Binh, Luu Minh Chau, Nguyen Lam, Hoang Manh Phu, Le Duc Chinh, Nguyen Van De, Nguyen Ngoc Khanh, Nguyen Tien Phong, and Nguyen Xuan Phong. In addition, there is a three-man administrative staff under the executive committee, composed of Truong Dinh Bang, Vu Huu Loan, and Phong Nha. While none of these names—except Vu Quang's—is well known, it is quite probable that some of the top Party leaders in the next generation will come from this group.

8. Party delegates came from these Communist-ruled countries: Albania, Bulgaria, Cuba, Czechoslovakia, the Democratic Republic of Germany, Hungary, Korea, Laos, Mongolia, Poland, Rumania, and the USSR. Communist Party representatives also came from Angola, Canada, Chile, Finland, France, Great Britain, Italy, Japan, Mexico, Mozambique, the Palestine Liberation Organization, Portugal, South Africa, Spain, Sweden, the United States (Henry Winston), and West Germany.

9. Continuing members: Le Duan, Truong Chinh, Pham Van Dong, Pham Hung, Le Duc Tho, Vo Nguyen Giap, Nguyen Duy Trinh, Le Thanh Nghi, Tran Quoc Hoan, and Van Tien Dung. New members were: Le Van Luong, Nguyen Van Cuc (alias Nguyen Van Linh), Vo Toan (alias Vo Chi Cong), and Chu Huy Man. New alternates: To Huu, Vo Van Kiet (alias Sau Dan), and Do Muoi.

Bibliography

(Foreign Languages Publishing House is cited as FLPH. All the Vietnamese periodicals and newspapers cited are published in Hanoi.)

Asprey, Robert B. *War in the Shadows: The Guerrilla in History.* 2 vols. New York: Doubleday & Co., 1975.

Berman, Paul. *Revolutionary Organization.* Lexington, Mass.: D. C. Heath & Co., Lexington Books, 1974.

Betts, Russel H. *Viet Cong Village Control.* Cambridge: M.I.T. Center for International Studies, 1969.

Bhandarsi, S. K. *Vietnam Today.* New Delhi: National Publications Bureau, 1964.

Burchette, Wilfred. *North of the 17th Parallel.* Hanoi: n.p., 1955.

Chen, King C. *Vietnam and China: 1938–54.* Princeton: Princeton University Press, 1969.

China News Analysis (Hong Kong).

China Quarterly. No. 9 (January–March 1962). Issue devoted to North Vietnam.

Conley, Michael. *The Communist Insurgent Infrastructure in South Vietnam: A Study of Organization and Strategy.* Department of the Army Pamphlet no. 550-160. Washington, D.C.: Center for Research in Social Systems, 1967.

———. "Communist Thought and Viet Cong Tactics." *Asian Survey,* March 1968.

Dang Dinh Giap. "The model Party member in North Vietnam." *Thoi su pho thong,* May 11, 1960.

Dang Lao Dong. *Breaking Our Chains: The August Revolution.* Hanoi: FLPH, 1960.

———. *Brief biography of Ho Chi Minh.* Hanoi: Nhan Dan Publishing House, 1970.

———. *Brief history of our Party and eight lessons of experience: faculty of Party history of Nguyen Ai Quoc School.* 2 vols. Hanoi: Tien Phong Publishing House, 1965.

———. "Bylaws of the Vietnam Lao Dong Youth Group." *Tien phong,* March 31, 1961.

———. "Circular on Party Central Committee directive on short-term theoretical and political education classes." *Tuyen huan,* July–August 1971.

———. *Communiqué of the Ninth Lao Dong Party Central Committee Session.* Hanoi: FLPH, 1964.

———. "The dictatorship of the proletariat will win total victory." *Hoc tap,* February 1971.

———. "Discipline in the Party." *Nhan dan,* January 28, 1962.

———. Forty-five Years of Activities of the Dang Lao Dong. Hanoi: FLPH, 1975.

———. General knowledge of the world and our country. Hanoi: Tien Phong Publishing House, 1966.

———. *A Heroic People: Memoirs from the Revolution.* Hanoi: FLPH, 1965.

———. *Historic Documents of the Lao Dong Party.* Reproduced by U.S. Joint Publications Research Service, JPRS 50557. Washington, D.C.: National Technical Information Service.

———. *History of the August Revolution.* Hanoi: Su That Publishing House, 1972.

———. "Ideological activities must be closely linked to organizational activities." *Tuyen huan,* July–August 1971.

———. *Our president, Ho Chi Minh.* Hanoi: FLPH, 1970.

———. *An Outline History of the Vietnam Workers Party, 1930–1970.* Hanoi: FLPH, 1970.

———. *Party documents, 1939–45.* Hanoi: Su That Publishing House, 1963.

———. *Party tasks and duties.* Hanoi: Quan Doi Nhan Dan Publishing House, 1972.

———. *President Ho Chi Minh.* Hanoi: FLPH, 1960.

———. "Resolution of the sixth congress of the central executive committee of the Vietnam Workers Youth League." *Tien phong,* February 16, 1959.

———. "Resolution on tasks related to cadres in the new phase." *Nhan dan,* March 12, 1973.

——. "Resolutions adopted at the national congress of the Lao Dong Youth Group." *Tien phong*, February 29, 1960.

——. "Study the Lao Dong Party Central Committee's Nineteenth Plenum resolution, 'On the dictatorship of the proletariat.' " *Thoi su pho thong*, September 9, 1971.

——. *Third National Congress of Vietnam Workers.* 3 vols. Hanoi: FLPH, 1960.

——. *Thirty Years of Struggle of the Party.* Hanoi: FLPH, 1960.

——. *Thirty-five Years of Struggle of the Party.* Hanoi: FLPH, 1965.

——. "Understanding the Party's history." *Thoi su pho thong*, January 4, 1970.

——. "Valiant struggle tradition of the Party's Youth Group." *Quan doi nhan dan*, February 28, 1966.

Dao Duy Can. "Party leadership in political training." *Nhan dan*, July 11, 1959.

[Democratic Republic of Vietnam.] *History of Vietnam.* Hanoi: Su That Publishing House, 1971.

——. Vietnam Studies. Hanoi: FLPH, 1964. No. 7, *Land Reform* [by Truong Phoung], 1966. No. 17, *Pages of History*, ca. 1968. No. 21, *Traditional Vietnam: Some Historical Stages*, ca. 1970. No. 24 (continuation of no. 21), *A Century of Struggles*, ca. 1971.

Devillers, Philippe. *Histoire du Vet Nam de 1940 à 1952.* Paris: Edition de Seuil, 1952.

Dorsenne, Jean. *Faudra-t-il évacuer l'Indochine?* Paris, 1932.

——. "Le peril rouge en Indochine." *Revue des deux mondes*, April 1, 1932.

Duc Thuan. "Understanding the historical mission of the Vietnamese working class before 1930." Hanoi: *Nghien cuu lich su*, March–April 1970.

Duiker, William J. *The Comintern and Vietnamese Communism.* Columbus: Ohio State University Center for International Studies, 1975.

——. "Ideology and Nation Building in the DRV." Xeroxed, 1976.

——. "The Red Soviets of Nghe Tinh: An Early Communist Rebellion in Vietnam." *Journal of Southeast Asia Studies*, no. 4 (September 1973).

——. "Revolutionary Youth League: Cradle of Communism in Viet Nam." China Quarterly, no. 53 (July–August 1972).

——. *The Rise of Nationalism in Vietnam: 1900–1941.* Ithaca: Cornell University Press, 1976.

Duncanson, Dennis J. *Government and Revolution in Vietnam.* London: Oxford University Press, 1968.

——. "Ho Chi Minh in Hong Kong, 1931–32." *China Quarterly*, 1975, no. 1.

Ennis, Thomas E. *French Policy and Developments in Indochina.* Chicago: University of Chicago Press, 1936.

Fall, Bernard B. "North Vietnam: A Profile." *Problems of Communism*, July–August 1965.

———. *The Two Vietnams: A Political and Military History*. 5th rev. ed. New York: Praeger Publishers, 1965.

———. *Le Viet Minh, 1945–60*. Paris: Librarie Armand Colin, 1960.

Fenn, Charles. *Ho Chi Minh: A Biographical Introduction*. New York: Charles Scribner's Sons, 1974.

Frei, Bruno. *Spring in Vietnam*. East Berlin, 1959.

Ginsburgs, George. "Local Government and Administration in North Vietnam, 1945–54." *China Quarterly*, no. 10 (April–June 1962) and no. 14 (April–June 1963).

Halberstam, David. *Ho*. New York: Random House, 1971.

Ho Chi Minh. *Democracy, discipline, and revolutionary ethics*. Rev. ed. Hanoi: Su That Publishing House, 1969.

———. *Prison Diary*. New York: Bantam Books, 1971.

———. *On Revolution: Selected Writings, 1920–66*. Edited and with an introduction by Bernard B. Fall. New York: Praeger Publishers, 1967.

———. *Selected Works: 1920–69*. Hanoi: FLPH, 1973.

———. *Selected Works: 1929–60*. 4 vols. Hanoi: Su That Publishing House, 1960; FLPH, 1960.

Hoa Mai, ed. *The Nhan Dan affair*. Saigon: Cong Hoa, 1968.

Hoang Minh Giam. "Improving the nature of the Party." *Hoc tap*, June 1967.

Hoang Quang Binh. "Meetings with Uncle in Yunnan." *Thoi moi*, May 1960.

Hoang Quoc Viet. "Lao Dong Party policy on enterprise management reform." *Nhan dan*, October 29, 1958.

Hoang Van Chi. *From Colonialism to Communism: A Case History of North Vietnam*. New York: Praeger Publishers, 1964.

———. ed. *The New Class in North Vietnam*. Saigon: Cong Dan, 1958.

Honey, P. J. *Communism in North Vietnam: Its Role in the Sino-Soviet Dispute*. Cambridge: M.I.T. Press, 1963.

———. "North Vietnam's Party Congress." *China Quarterly*, no. 4 (October–December 1960).

———, ed. *North Vietnam Today: Profile of a Communist Satellite*. Cambridge: M.I.T. Press, 1962.

Hong Chuong. "Bourgeois and proletarian democracies: bourgeois democracy is sham democracy." *Quan doi nhan dan*, April 22, 1976.

———. "On the matter of Communists and Nationalists." *Thong nhat*, February 26, 1971.

———. "The state's persuasive and coercive methods." *Hoc tap*, February 1976.

Huynh Kim Khanh. "The Vietnamese August Revolution Reinterpreted." *Journal of Asian Studies*, no. 4 (August 1971).

Joint U.S. Public Affairs Office (JUSPAO). Documents and Research Notes. Saigon: U.S. Mission, 1965–73. No. 84, *Brief Chronology of Momentous Facts and Events in the History of the DRV, 1945–70*, 1970. No. 96, *Vietnam Workers Party 1963 Decision to Escalate the War in the South*, 1971. No. 102, *People's Revolutionary Party of South Vietnam*, 1972.

———. *The New Statute on Agricultural Cooperatives*. Saigon: U.S. Mission, 1969.

———. *Vietnamese Communist Leadership*. Saigon: U.S. Mission, ca. 1970.

Lacouture, Jean. *Ho Chi Minh: A Political Biography*. New York: Random House, 1968.

Lancaster, Donald. *The Emancipation of French Indochina*. London: Oxford University Press, 1961.

Langer, Paul, and Zasloff, Joseph J. *North Vietnam and the Pathet Lao: Partners in the Struggle for Laos*. Cambridge: Harvard University Press, 1970.

Le Duan. *Forward under the Glorious Banner of the October Revolution*. Hanoi: FLPH, 1967.

———. *The Socialist Revolution in Vietnam*. Hanoi: FLPH, 1957.

———. *On the Socialist Revolution in Vietnam*. 3 vols. Hanoi: FLPH, 1965–66.

———. *On Some Present International Problems*. Hanoi: FLPH, 1964.

———. *South Vietnam Revolutionary Path*. Publisher unknown, ca. 1956.

———. *The Vietnamese Revolution: Fundamental Problems, Essential Tasks*. Hanoi: FLPH, 1970.

Le Duc Binh. "Party development must be closely linked to the development of the state and mass organizations." *Hoc tap*, January 1976.

Le Manh Trinh. "Meetings with Uncle Ho in Canton and Siam." *Tien phong*, May 18, 20, and 23, 1960.

Le Sy Thang. "President Ho and the introduction of Marxism-Leninism into Vietnam. *Nghien cuu lich su*, May–June and July–August 1972.

Leites, Nathan. *Viet Cong Style of Politics*. Santa Monica, Calif.: Rand Corp., 1969.

McGarvey, P. J., ed. *Visions of Victory: Selected Vietnamese Communist Military Writings*. Stanford: Stanford University Press, 1969.

McLane, Charles B. *Soviet Strategies in Southeast Asia: An Exploration of Eastern Policy under Lenin and Stalin*. Princeton: Princeton University Press, 1966.

Mau, Michael P. "The Training of Cadres in the Lao Dong Party of North Vietnam, 1960–67." *Asian Survey*, March 1967.

Nguyen Luong Bang. "First days of the August Revolution." *Tien phong*, May 6, 1960.

Nguyen Chuong. "The nature and mission of the Lao Dong Party." *Nhan dan*, April 15, 1960.

———. "Qualifications and traits of a Communist Party member." *Thoi su pho thong*, January 6, 1960.

———. "Understand the basic spirit of the revision of the Party statutes." *Nhan dan*, April 8, 1960.

Nguyen Duong. "Guide for district-level cadre training: concerning the line of the socialist revolution. *Tuyen huan*, March 1972.

Nguyen Duy Trinh and Pham Van Dong. *Problems Facing the DRV in 1961.* Hanoi: FLPH, 1961.

Nguyen Khac Huyen. *Vision Accomplished? The Enigma of Ho Chi Minh.* New York: MacMillan Co., Collier Books, 1971.

Nguyen Khac Vien. *The Long Resistance: 1858–1975.* Hanoi: FLPH, 1975.

———. ed. *Century of National Struggle: 1847–1945.* Hanoi: FLPH, 1969.

Nguyen Van Vinh. "Vietnam Lao Dong Party: organizer and leader of victory." *Thoi su pho thong*, January 6, 1960.

———. *The Vietnamese People on the Road to Victory.* Hanoi: FLPH, 1966.

O'Neil, Robert J. *General Giap: Politician and Strategist.* New York: Praeger Publishers, 1969.

Osborne, Milton. "Continuity and Motivation in the Vietnamese Revolution: New Light from the 1930's." *Pacific Affairs*, Spring 1974.

Pham Van Dong. *Ho Chi Minh: A Political Biography.* Hanoi: FLPH, 1969.

———. "Lenin and the revolutionary struggle of our people." *Nhan dan*, April 22, 1960.

———. *Our Struggle in the Past and at the Present.* Hanoi: FLPH, 1955.

Pike, Douglas. *Communist Party of South Vietnam.* Saigon: U.S. Mission, 1966.

———. *Viet Cong: The Organization and Techniques of the National Liberation Front of South Vietnam.* Cambridge: M.I.T. Press, 1966.

———. *Viet Cong Strategy of Terror.* Saigon: U.S. Mission, 1970.

———. "Vietnam War: Major Events and Nature and Character." In *Marxism, Communism, and Western Society: A Comparative Encyclopedia*, edited by C. D. Kernig. Freiburg: Verlag Herder, 1973.

———. *War, Peace, and the Viet Cong.* Cambridge: M.I.T. Press, 1969.

———, ed. "History of the Vietnam War on Microfilm." 9 vols. In preparation. Vol. 5: DRV/LD 68, "Party Cadre Handbook: Communism Is the Ultimate Goal of Our Party" (1968). VCD 21, "Primer of Vietnamese Communism" (ca. 1962). VCD 43, "Standard Requirements for a Communist Party Member" (ca. 1962). VCD 134, "Lao Dong Party Membership Requirements Adjusted for Use in the South" (1962).

Porter, Gareth. *A Peace Denied.* Bloomington: Indiana University Press, 1976.

Rambo, Terry. *A Comparison of Peasant Social Systems of North and South Vietnam.* Carbondale: Southern Illinois University Press, 1973.

Republic of Vietnam Armed Forces (RVNAF) Joint Chiefs of Staff. *North Vietnam Country Study.* Saigon, 1974.

Sacks, I. Milton. "Communism and Nationalism in Vietnam, 1918–1946." Ph.D. diss., Yale University, 1959. (Available at U.S. Department of State Library.)

———. "Marxism in Vietnam." In *Marxism in Southeast Asia,* edited by Frank N. Trager. Stanford: Stanford University Press, 1965.

———. *Political Alignments of Vietnamese Nationalists.* U.S. Department of State, Office of Intelligence and Research report OIR 3708. Washington, D.C., 1949.

Sainteny, Jean. *Ho Chi Minh and His Vietnam: A Personal Memoir.* Chicago: Cowles Book Co., 1972.

SEATO. *Principal Institutions and Personalities of North Vietnam.* Rev. ed. Bangkok: SEATO, 1973.

Smith, Harvey H., et al. *Area Handbook for North Vietnam.* Washington, D.C.: Government Printing Office, 1967.

Song Le. "The mass line of the Party." *Hoc tap,* August–September 1960.

Staar, Richard F., ed. *Aspects of Modern Communism.* Columbia: University of South Carolina Press, 1969.

———. *Yearbook on International Communist Affairs.* Stanford: Hoover Institution Press, 1972–77.

Steibel, Gerald L. "Communist Expansion in Indochina." *Southeast Asian Perspectives,* December 1972.

Tanham, George K. *Communist Revolutionary Warfare: The Vietminh in Indochina.* New York: Praeger Publishers, 1961.

Thayer, Carlyle A. *Revolutionary Elites in Southern Viet-Nam: Political Biography.* Melbourne: University of Melbourne, 1976.

———. "Socialist Construction in the DRV: Agricultural Collectivization, 1957–70." Xeroxed, 1971.

———. "The Socializing Environment of Vietnamese Revolutionaries, 1909–1958." Xeroxed, ca. 1971.

To Hoai. "President Ho, the father of the Vietnamese revolutionary army." *Nhan dan,* May 15, 1960.

Trager, Frank. "Viet Nam: The Origin and Development of Communism to 1966." *Pacific Community*, no. 7 (Summer 1970).

Tran Huy Lieu. "The historical significance of the Third Party Congress." *Nghien cuu lich su*, December 1960.

———. "Nguyen Ai Quoc, leader of the Party of the Vietnamese working class." *Lao dong*, May 19, 1960.

Tran Ngac Dang. "Leadership of the basic Party organization in the ground officers school." *Quan doi nhan dan*, September 23–25, 1958.

Tran Ngan. "Several experiences in supervising Party development activity." *Hoc tap*, March 1976.

Tran Van Giau. *The Ideological Development of Vietnam from the Early Nineteenth Century to the August Revolution*. Hanoi: Social Sciences Publishing House, 1973.

———. "The Party and the working class." *Lao dong*, December 19, 1959.

Truong Buu Lam. *Patterns of Vietnamese Response to Foreign Intervention, 1858–1900*. New Haven: Yale University Press, 1967.

Truong Chinh. *The August Revolution*. 2d ed. Hanoi: FLPH, 1962.

———. *Forward along the Path Charted by Karl Marx*. Hanoi: FLPH, 1969.

———. *President Ho Chi Minh: Beloved Leader of the Vietnamese People*. Hanoi: FLPH, 1966.

———. *The Resistance Will Win*. Hanoi: FLPH, 1960.

———. *Resolutely Taking the North Vietnam Countryside to Socialism*. Hanoi: FLPH, 1969.

——— and Vo Nguyen Giap. *The Peasant Question: 1937–38*. Translated by Christine Pelzer White. Cornell University Southeast Asia Program Data Paper no. 94. Ithaca, 1974.

Turley, William S. "Civil-Military Relations in North Vietnam." *Asian Survey*, December 1969.

Turner, Robert F. *Vietnamese Communism: Its Origins and Development*. Stanford: Hoover Institution Press, 1975.

U.S. Dept. of State. Foreign Area Research Documents. FAR 20257. "Building the United Front: The Communist Movement in Vietnam, 1930–54" [by William J. Duiker]. Washington, D.C.

U.S., Department of State. *Working Papers on North Vietnam's Role in the War in South Vietnam*. Washington, D.C., 1968.

Van Dyke, Jon M. *North Vietnam's Strategy for Survival*. Palo Alto, Calif.: Pacific Books, 1972.

Vo Nguyen Giap. *Arm the Revolutionary Masses to Build the People's Army*. Hanoi: FLPH, 1975.

————. *Big Victory, Great Task.* Hanoi: FLPH, 1967.

————. *Dien Bien Phu.* 2d ed. Hanoi: FLPH, 1962.

————. *People's War against U.S. Aero-Naval War.* Hanoi: FLPH, 1975.

————. *People's War, People's Army.* Hanoi: FLPH, 1961.

————. *Unforgettable Days: August 1945–December 1946.* Hanoi: FLPH, 1975.

Vo Tri Huu. "How to carry out the 'chi bo' congresses well." *Nhan dan,* April 19, 1960.

Vu Anh. "Uncle Ho returns from Kunming." *Lao dong,* May 14, 1960.

Vu Huy Phuc. "Reflections about the working class in the first years under the leadership of the ICP." Hanoi: *Nghien cuu lich su,* March–April 1970.

Vu Ngoc Khanh. "Propagandizing Leninism in Vietnam prior to the August Revolution." *Tuyen huan,* July–August 1970.

Vu Tho. "Election of provincial and district Lao Dong Party committees in North Vietnam." *Nhan dan,* December 29, 1958.

Warbey, William. *Ho Chi Minh.* London: Merlin Press, 1972.

White, Christine Pelzer. *Land Reform in North Vietnam.* Washington, D.C.: Agency for International Development, 1970.

Woodside, Alexander B. *Community and Revolution in Modern Vietnam.* New York: Houghton Mifflin Co., 1976.

Zagoria, Donald. *Vietnam Triangle: Moscow, Peking, and Hanoi.* New York: Pegasus, 1967.

Zasloff, J. J. *Political Motivation of the Viet Cong.* Rev. ed. Santa Monica, Calif.: Rand Corp., 1968.

————, and Brown, MacAlister, eds. *Communism in Indochina: New Perspectives.* Lexington, Mass.: D. C. Heath & Co., Lexington Books, 1975.

Index

Accords: Geneva, 87–88; Paris, 120
Annam Communist Party, *see* Annam Cong San Dang
Annam Cong San Dang, 8
Anti-Imperialist League, *see* Hoi Dong Minh Phan De
Armed struggle, 18, 21, 116–17
August Revolution, 51–54

Bao Dai, 51, 52, 76, 87, 3n.5
Bazin, M., 26
Bi Ap Buc Dan Toc Lien Hiep Hoi, 2
Blum, Leon, 57
Borodin, Mikhail, 2, 56, 57, 59
Buddhism, 31–32, 80
Bui Quang Chieu, 81
Buttinger, Joseph, 1n.1, 2n.2

Cachin, Marcel, 56–57
Cadre, 67–71
Cao Dai, 30–31, 44, 53, 80, 94
Cao Vong Thanh Nien Dang, 29
Catholics, *see* Roman Catholic Church
Chen, King, 5n.2
China, relation of Party, 1, 3, 6, 14, 104–6, 130–32, 148–49
Ching Fa-kwei, 45–47
Chou En-lai, 57, 63
Chu Huy Man, 8n.9
Chu Van Tan, 48, 52, 82, 3n.4
Cole, Allan B., 5n.10

Comintern, 9, 17, 19, 33, 34
Communist Youth Group, *see* Thanh Nien Cong San Doan
Communist Youth League, *see* Thanh Nien Cong San Doan
Constitutional Party, 81
Cuong De, 28, 30
Cuu Quoc, 45, 94

Dai Viet, 27–28, 81–82
Dai Viet Dan Chinh, 44
Dai Viet Quoc Dan Dang, 28, 44, 53, 81–82, 2n.16, 5n.8
Dan Xa Social Democratic Party, 31
Dang Cong San Dong Duong, 12, 15, 73, 77, 83, 89, 1n.15, 3n.2
Dang Cong San Vietnam, 121, 134, 146–148
Dang Nhan Dan Cach Mang, 121–123, 125–126
Dang Thai Mai, 62
De Pouvourillive, Albert, 16
Devillers, Philippe, 5n.9
Do Muoi, 83, 8n.9
Do Ngoc Du, 6, 8, 66
Do Quang Giai, 2n.19
Dong Du, 28
Dong Duong Cong San Lien Doan, 8
Dong Minh Hoi, *see* Viet Nam Cach Mang Dong Minh Hoi
Dong Van Cong, 124
Duiker, William J., 1nn.1, 2; 4n.6

3000 PB